Ordinary Awakenings

How to Discover Valuable Gifts in Life's Ordinary Experiences

D0291121

Kathy M. Irr

Blessings,

Kathy M. Irr

Husky Trail Press LLC

Copyright © 2014 Kathy M. Irr

kemi24@juno.com
www.kathymirr.com

ISBN 978-1-935258-22-3

Cover and chapter images by Kathy M. Irr

Husky Trail Press LLC
PO Box 705
153 Boston Post Road, #L
East Lyme, CT 06333

Printed in the United States of America.

Dedication

For my **Dziadziu**, who
taught me the importance of the
power of presence.

To my parents **John** and **Bernice**, who taught me what it means to love and be loved unconditionally. You've never waivered.

To my sisters, **Donna**, **Teresa**, **Joanne**, **Patti**, and **Mary**, and my brother **John**, who have been my best friends in life.

To my husband, **Frank**, who has supported all my dreams. I could not have done it without you. It's not always been an easy journey, but it has been a beautiful one, and keeps getting better!

And to my sons, **Michael** and **Christopher**, who make me proud not only because they pursue their dreams, but in that pursuit, they remain faith-filled and compassionate men.

I will love you all forever!

Acknowledgments

Special thanks to my editor Debby Adams who helped shape my message. My thanks to Richard LaPorta, my publisher, who walked me through this process, putting my mind at ease each step along the way. To my spiritual director Bob McNally who creates sacred space for me to safely share my spiritual journey. To my life coach Marcus Milukas who never accepted, "I don't know" as an answer and instead encouraged me to dig deeper. I am grateful to my "Good Morning Friends" who lovingly allowed me to share reflections with them for a year. Your encouragement helped me to grow. Thank you to all the wonderful friends in Portsmouth, Monterey, New Orleans, Burke, and Kodiak who shared our ports of call. Those memories will last a lifetime. To my former colleagues and students who invited me to share in their laughter, sorrow, struggles, and joys, I'm forever grateful.

We all need "cheerleaders" and so I offer thanks to members of my church community who encourage me at every turn. I extend my gratitude to Twelve Step friends who introduced me to a relationship with God that has no boundaries. In loving gratitude to all of the Zawada, Morrissey and Irr families, your love and support mean so much to me. To my mentors at Our Lady of Calvary, Genesis Spiritual Life Center, Immaculata Retreat Center, Mercy Center and Enders Island, thank you for giving me opportunities to continue the learning process and to share my ministry with others.

I am grateful to you if our paths have crossed, whether the experience was one of joy or struggle; I've learned something with each encounter.

Contents

Chapters in Alphabetical Order

Introduction

"If you allow yourself to be formed by God through the common, ordinary, unspectacular flow of everyday life, you will gradually experience a liberation and freedom never before imagined. Stand ready to answer when asked if you are available for God to become more present in your life and through you to the world."
Theodore James Ryken

My spiritual journey and relationship with God intensified and became increasingly more fruitful when I began, over thirty years ago, to write my thoughts and feelings in journals. As part of my recovery process from addiction, it was suggested that I write as often as possible, reflecting on the very ordinary experiences of my days. This gave me glimpses of insight, wisdom, and understanding into my own spiritual hunger for God's presence in my life. Each reflection provided the impetus to search more deeply so that I would, first and foremost, always dwell in God. Simply put, I desired God to be at the center of my life. From that place of God-centeredness, all understanding and grace could be welcomed.

There is a spiritual energy that connects each of us to one another and to every living thing in our universe. God's desire is for us to shine forth our positive energy and light to the world around us. This energy and light comes to us as gift. As with all gifts, it is an opportunity to recognize, receive, and to re-gift this energy and light to others. There is an incredible joy that comes when we become seekers of truth and light.

Wouldn't it be wonderful if in the midst of our ordinary experiences we could find God's movements within them? Whatever your present circumstances, reading this book can spark ideas, encourage questions, and generate responses that will help you to strengthen and renew your spiritual growth.

Perhaps, you are curious about where your spiritual path is leading. If at present you feel confused or feel as though you've not experienced a connection with God, these stories and reflections are especially meant for you. The fact that you are reading this book tells me that you, like me, desire intimacy with a loving Power greater than yourself. This relationship takes form over the course of our entire lifetime. It happens when we are feeling strong and when we are at our most vulnerable. Every day is an opportunity to find God in the most ordinary and mundane circumstances of life.

You are invited to read and listen with your heart. God receives you right where you are, whatever your present circumstances. If it's inner peace and joy that you are seeking, this may be a great place to start.

Let me make it clear from the very start that we all struggle some days to find the joy and peace God offers. Our journey is not an easy one; however, I've discovered that difficulties and challenges do not make for a joyless journey. As a matter of fact, as we discover the gifts hidden within our trials, indeed, the world is full of great potential and possibility. It is our perspective in life that makes all the difference. The choice to be happy is up to us. God pursues us with a passion, and although we often become sidetracked by worldly distractions, God is always inviting us to refocus our attention on what matters most in life. If we center ourselves in God (Love), we can remain at peace despite chaos, stressful moments, and dry periods in our lives. This book offers a way to focus in on the gifts found in our ordinary experiences.

Jean Baptiste Girard once said, "By words we learn thoughts, and by thoughts we learn life." Words then, offer us an opportunity to deepen our faith life. We can contemplate the meaning of written words and choose to act upon them or not. As we become aware of God's presence at the center of our lives, those words can move us to act in accordance with God's will for us. Think for a moment how the powerful words of scripture, spiritual writers, mentors, and religious leaders have transformed lives throughout history.

As we contemplate words and their meanings in our lives, stories begin to unfold. At their best, words move us to tears, spur us to action, heal wounds, comfort, give meaning to our feelings, and expression to our prayers. Words help us to remain connected to each other. We type them, text them, say them, write them, advertise them, read them, act them out, and process them.

My intention in writing this book is to encourage you to go deeper to discover God's daily invitation to become the person you are called to be. As you become increasingly mindful of God's light shining within you, you give expression to that light in the world around you. Listen for the voice, the nudges and intuitions that are inspired by the Spirit working in and through you. I remind people all the time that it's not about doing things the way I or anyone else does them; it's important to find ways that work best for you. The stories and reflections in this book may help you to find your own ways of communicating with God and noticing God's presence in life's most ordinary experiences.

As you will find out in some of my stories, the experiences and circumstances of my life that have led to a deeper and more intimate relationship with God weren't always welcome with open arms. If there was an "easier and softer way" to peace and contentment, I looked for it!

Believe me—there are times we all want to run away and hide from painful and complicated experiences. In the end, attempts to avoid the process seem to prolong the discomfort. Learning to accept whatever experiences or circumstances come our way is part of a maturing spiritual life. We won't always understand it, and it doesn't always feel good, but once we acknowledge and accept our present reality, we have the opportunity to work through it with God's guidance and support. I encourage you to go easy on yourself as you journey to reveal the person God is calling you to be. You may encounter obstacles such as fear, stubbornness, apathy, disbelief, and the like. Don't give up; you are among saints and sinners, ancestors and mentors who have been down this same spiritual path. Allow yourself to receive grace. If you feel closed to it, know that God gives it freely and even your best attempts to reject it are not bigger than God's desire for you to have it.

This book is about opening ourselves up to the possibilities of change, not by forcing ourselves to do so, but rather by paying attention to our responses and attitudes toward the simple, ordinary experiences of our daily life. Rather than being changed by this book, I hope it shines a light on the wonderful abilities and gifts just waiting to emerge from within you. Rarely is it lack of opportunities that come our way; rather it is a matter of noticing them and making the choice to act on them, perhaps with a new perspective.

I did not intend for this book to be read cover to cover in several hours or days. It does not unfold in one continuous story. In the following chapters, you will read quotes, stories, and reflections that give some insight into my personal journey.

My suggestion is to take small "bites" and sit with your thoughts or feelings. Hopefully, what I share with you is a catalyst that helps ignite your own personal responses. Keep in mind that spiritual growth is a process. Give yourself time to pause and reflect on what it is you are feeling in response to a word, story, or reflection. Use the questions to help you probe a little deeper into better understanding yourself in relationship to God and others.

Begin by choosing a word from the chapter list. Sit quietly and repeat the word several times in your mind. Center yourself on this one word and let God reveal something about its meaning to you. If you wish to write down some thoughts, this would be an excellent time to do so.

Next, read the quote and again let the words and meaning speak to you. Remember that each person will interpret what they are reading and feeling in different ways. Your experiences, desires, and present circumstances will help determine your response. There is no right or wrong response.

Following the quote, read the personal story and reflection. Let the words settle into the sacred space within your body. Trust me—sacred space exists within all of us; it is a matter of tapping into it. Savor each one of your reflection periods. Ask God to focus your attention on anything that is important for you.

The reflection questions are to help you become more aware of how your life may or may not be thriving in regard to your present relationship with God, others, and yourself. This is an opportunity to explore new insights. Do not use your time to berate yourself. Look honestly and fairly, without passing judgments.

Whether you decide to write your responses or use it as a mental exercise, continue to keep the focus on your chosen word. The following questions may help you to remain focused on the word or theme that is unfolding as you are reading.

- What meaning does this word hold in my life today?
- Where and how do I experience the meaning of this word? How does it play out in my daily experiences?
- What opportunities are available for me to act on the meaning of this word?
- As I understand the meaning of this word, am I experiencing any resistance or lack of willingness to either receive or act on it?
- How does this word have meaning as I journey onward in my spiritual growth?

Does this process of reflection really work to improve our conscious contact with God? The answer is, "Yes, absolutely!" if you are willing to practice digging into these words and their meanings for your life. Feel free to add more words to your spiritual reflections. There is so much potential for growth just waiting below the surface. God is excited, waiting to reveal gifts to you that you've yet to imagine.

Your responses and personal reflections help to make you more aware of the gift you are to the world. They remind you to reflect your inner light to all those you encounter in your daily comings and goings. It's not about an out-of-body spiritual awakening, but rather the stuff of everyday life.

Brene Brown, an author and speaker, once described stories as "data with a soul." Words are what make up the story. We can open ourselves up and pay closer attention to the words and their meaning in our daily lives. As we willingly shift our focus, we can better connect with God, others, and the natural world around us. Our experiences will become richer and more meaningful as we pay closer attention to the data.

Keep an open mind and allow these simple stories and reflections to resonate within you. I don't need to tell you what to do; you will intuitively know. A caution, especially for the novice explorer: the "knowing" may not come in the form of lightning bolts, but, rather, slowly over time. If I've learned anything, it is that spiritual growth demands *patience*. If you don't have patience, pray for it *now*!!!! (We have to be able to laugh at ourselves! Humor is most valuable to the process.)

No matter where you are in your spiritual journey, I invite you to be mindful of the present. Do not set yourself up with expectations. Allow the Spirit to direct the movement. The God of Mystery and Surprise is waiting to connect ever more deeply within you.

Kathy M. Irr

Chapter I

Acceptance

*"Accepting and blessing our circumstances
is a powerful tool for transformation."*
Sarah Ban Breathnach

It is difficult to imagine that given the opportunities, gifts, and talents God had given me, I was actually thinking at the age of twenty-one that life was too difficult to bear. My childhood was filled with unconditional love and acceptance, support, security, and opportunities galore. Somehow, though, in this moment, those memories seemed to be overshadowed by despair. My food addiction engulfed my being and seemed to swallow me whole. While I was battling the "dis-ease" of compulsive eating, of binging and starving, food was becoming my god. Many young people my age were also battling this disease. Most of us suffered in silence, believing we should be able to handle the problem on our own. I felt very isolated and alone. Although I put on a good front, my insides were crumbling in desperation, and I was feeling totally out of control.

As a young woman, I had little understanding of what it meant to accept and bless the circumstances of my life. All I knew was that I *was dealing with my inner turmoil alone, and I wanted it to stop. My greatest desire was to feel normal like everyone else! I didn't want to worry about what others thought of me or what I thought of myself. The self-judgment was overwhelming. I desperately wanted to relax and enjoy my life. I was tired of hiding and pretending. My dream of becoming a nurse was coming true, and yet there was so much doubt.*

One day, I stood at a street corner waiting for the light to change so I could cross over to the hospital, go to the surgical floor, and locate my patients for the following day. This was a typical routine for nursing students in training, although this particular evening my heart and mind was burdened and preoccupied.

As I stood waiting, I began thinking that if a semi-truck hit me, it would end my misery. I knew I wouldn't commit suicide, but at that moment, I sure thought it seemed easier than the emotional, physical, and spiritual weight I was carrying inside of me.

It wasn't until several years later when I accepted that I used food as comfort, to push down emotions, to calm anxieties, and to satisfy powerful desires within my brain, that I was able to begin on a road to wellness of mind, body and spirit.

Transformation is possible only when we accept our circumstances as they are. There are times when we feel broken, sick, tired, and scared. It is in our vulnerability that we can pray for God to help us. We finally give up trying to control what is impossible to control. We admit that we need God and others in our life to support us through the difficult times. We are willing to go to whatever lengths it takes to be well. We surrender old habits and give up on ideas that no longer serve us well. We listen to people who've been in our shoes, and accept their support, unconditional love, and guidance. We realize God is answering our prayers.

If we remain willing to ask for help and then listen to the wisdom given to us, we come to realize what a blessing those difficult circumstances have been to us. Buried in the pain are invaluable gifts that completely change our attitude, disposition, and outlook on life. Our life's work and dreams are possible because of what we've experienced in our lives. Our relationship with God and others continues to unfold and strengthen. We are filled with hope and possibilities today.

Living in Alaska for a period of time gave me the opportunity to climb some rather challenging mountain trails. One day I decided to take a two-hour hike for my exercise. The seemingly calm weather shifted as I began my climb up the mountain. As my legs tired and my breath labored in the strong wind I thought about abandoning my hike and returning home. I assessed the situation and decided that perhaps I could change my perspective. Shifting my goals and expectations allowed me to take whatever the mountain was offering this day. My pace slowed. I heard the winds whispering. Rather than exercise, I was on an excursion. My goal was no longer to reach the summit but to linger in the beauty of the space around me. I was able to refocus myself in the presence of the banquet that was lying before me.

What stands in the way of personal peace and serenity? Is there something that is blocking our relationship with God, others or the world around us? It's important to ask ourselves if we've become negatively attached to anything in our daily lives that does not allow us to attain God's deepest desires for us?

Gerald May, in his book *Addiction and Grace* states, "addiction exists wherever persons are internally compelled to give energy to things that are not their true desires." He goes on to refer to attachment as "…the process that enslaves desire and creates a state of addiction." May's reference to "attachment" helps everyone to understand that our world is rife with attachments. Drugs, alcohol, and food are but a few of the attachments to which we can become enslaved. If we begin to cling to and make anything more important than God then we have become negatively attached. This includes, but is not limited to: material things, institutions, people, beliefs, power, control, sex, money, and worry. If we begin to look with a new set of eyes, there are a multitude of temptations that we begin to recognize as attachments.

Don't misunderstand; it's not that there can be no pleasure in the "things" of this world, but when we become attached to them and begin to use them to satisfy our own needs at the expense of others, we may be negatively attached. Saint Ignatius in his *Spiritual Exercises* emphasizes that our purpose in life is to praise, reverence, and serve God. There is no way we can fully live out our life's purpose when we are negatively attached to people, places, or things.

Accepting and blessing our circumstances is the key to change. No matter how many attempts we make to change our behaviors, we cannot do it alone. If our desire is to realize our full God-given potential, then we must learn to first accept the realities of our life. We cannot change what we are unwilling to see. When we center ourselves in God and allow the plans and dreams of our Creator to flow out from within, rather than being forced by external or our own demands into roles that are not of God, we are set free.

Liking our circumstances and accepting them aren't necessarily one and the same. We don't have the viewpoint God does. We are often mired in the minutiae of temporary discomfort. That is understandable, especially in times of stress, loss, loneliness, and confusion. God sees and understands the big picture and holds us in those moments when we may feel lost. Accepting our circumstances means we are willing to surrender ourselves to the present moment, trusting God to take us through it. We stand before God humbly giving all of ourselves to this Holy Power. Often, people mistake surrender for giving in or giving up. Surrendering ourselves to God, in fact, opens us up to infinite possibilities. We are saying "yes" to God's plan rather than going it alone. The truth is, the world can be unkind and challenging. It can also be peaceful and joyful. God is with us through it all. As Jesus accepted his circumstances and trusted God to be with him, so too, we are called to do the same.

We begin by accepting that we don't have all the answers. We will need to ask for help. We aren't meant to go it alone. Asking questions is a great way for us to keep an open mind. It helps us to remain teachable. It allows us to seek out God's will for us.

- Make a list of the negative attachments that seem to be holding you back from fully experiencing joy and peace in your life.

- Honestly assess where it is you can possibly make positive changes and in prayer ask God to give you the willingness to do so.

- Talk to God as if talking to a trusted friend. A prayer can make all the difference. There are many prayers one can pray, but in the end it's better to keep it simple. If your concept of God does not lend you to trust Him, seek out someone to help you, a spiritual advisor or a trusted mentor.

- Notice those things that you have no control over. Stop trying to control what is impossible. Rather, talk with God and ask that you receive the strength and courage to let go of what you cannot change. It takes practice, practice, practice. Tell God as often as necessary, "I turn this over to you, and I'm willing to accept your guidance!" Be patient and persevere.

Sometimes we say we believe in God, but what does that really mean to us? Do we believe simply because we were raised to believe? Are we giving a lot of lip service to God while our hearts really are not trusting? It's easy to fall victim to the false idea that a God of such immense power cannot be bothered with our mundane problems and attachments enough to relieve us of them, especially when we think we should be able to handle them on our own. It is time for self-criticism to be replaced with self-acceptance.

Accepting the process of renewal and rediscovery continues to be a gift. Hidden within the circumstances and experiences of our attachments are these beautiful gifts we never dream exist. God's plans are sufficient for our lives. We can expand our capacity to accept life as it comes to us rather than having pie-in-the-sky expectations. There is no shame in asking for help. Thinking we know it all doesn't mean we do. Continuing to ask questions and to live with the questions is more important than having all the answers. Each day has hidden gifts ready to be revealed. You may discover that many of those gifts are revealed within times of difficulty and struggle as well as times of blessings and joy. If God is so willing to keep pursuing us, how willing are we to reciprocate in order to have God's deepest desires for us fulfilled?

PERSONAL REFLECTION

What role does acceptance play in your life today?

What is it you have to accept in your life in order to become that person whom God is calling you to be?

For what daily blessings are you grateful? What blessings have surfaced beneath the muck of life? How have these blessings changed or inspired you?

What questions, thoughts, reflections arise in you at this time?

Chapter 2

Surrender

*"The reason why many [of us] are still troubled,
still seeking, still making little forward progress
is because [we] haven't yet come to the end of [ourselves].
We're still trying to give orders,
and interfering with God's work within us."*
A. W. Tozer

Being the first-born, I was not typically the thrill-seeker or risk-taker in the family. However, on this particular summer day in the Adirondacks, the Spirit showed me how delightful it is to surrender ourselves to God's whimsy!

Up before the crack of dawn I readied myself to begin the day. It was a glorious morning in upstate New York; cool and crisp, I looked forward to my three-mile jog into town. Upon arrival at the local marina, I watched a beautiful sunrise while I stretched my body and prepared for my walk back to the lake house. Upon arrival back at the house, no one was stirring, so I decided to take the kayak out on the lake. The loons were whistling and the ducks swimming along side as I paddled my way around the lake. Upon my return, I thought, "OK, my exercise

19

is done for the day. Now I'll pull up a lounge chair, get a good book, and relax all day!"

In the late afternoon, I joined my husband and sister for a swim over to an island that was quite a distance from shore. This swim may not seem like a big deal to most. However, for a gal who, as a child, placed plastic bags on her feet to avoid contact with the bottom of the lake and all the creepy-crawlies in it; it was a huge deal. And swimming is not really my strong suit, no pun intended.

After reaching shore, invigorated and exhausted by the swim to and from the island, I had one more unexpected adventure. Returning to our kayaks, we crossed the lake to yet another island where a rope swing provided hours of fun for the teenage group among us. As we approached the island I heard the invitation, "Come on, Auntie Kathy, just try it!" I basically told my nephews they were "out of their minds!" Then, as I watched, something came over me and I found myself thinking, "why not?"

I rowed my kayak to the shore of the thickly rooted, pine-dotted island. I hopped out and began to ascend to the top of the platform set firmly into the bank of the island. After a short lesson in how to swing out—hold my arms tight to my body and lift my legs to my chest—I thought I was ready. Despite a chokehold on the rope, my mind was having difficulty letting my body go. Finally, I closed my eyes, counted to three, several times and jumped. As momentum carried me downward, I let go, and did a tremendous face plant right into the water!

After assuring everyone I was just fine, the roars of laughter ensued. I could only imagine the sight they had just witnessed. And guess what? I laughed with them. Then, I got back on that rope, and again, hit the water with a bang!

My rope jumping days are probably over, but it felt so good taking the risk. It wasn't only the physical risk I'm speaking of, rather the emotional and spiritual risk.

This day was about surrendering myself to the movement of the Spirit inside of me. Years of bad tapes that often played in my head were silenced. Chains of self-judgment were loosened. Fears dissipated in the joy of each moment and challenge. I was able to swim in the lake with all the creepy-crawlies. Getting out of that kayak in front of young men and my brother-in-laws in a bathing suit was a risk. I wasn't thinking about the cellulite on my wobbly legs and how I looked. While holding that rope, I didn't allow shear panic to incapacitate me and I kept my sense of humor.

As we all kayaked back across the lake toward home, we watched the most magnificent sunset. The day was amazing. I felt so free. My insides felt as glorious as the fiery sky upon which I gazed. My sister looked over and said, "We might as well enjoy every minute we have!" I thought about the truth of that statement. I don't want to live my life saying, "I wish I had." Instead, I want to surrender myself to a God of Surprises.

From sunup to sundown, I said, "Yes!" to living life to the fullest. I allowed myself to surrender the fear and doubts. I will take the experience of my lake adventures with me into my "everydays." I realize there will be days in the future that won't feel as exciting. If my attitude is one of surrender, I will open myself to whatever life has in store for me and will continue to look for simple grace and blessings in ordinary experiences.

A call to surrender is a call from the Beloved to be purely one with Him. It is a faith-filled response of complete trust in what is.

Our willingness to surrender to God is an act of love. At times it may feel a bit scary. Facing the unknown leaves us feeling vulnerable. We spend a lot of time fighting the "what-ifs" because it may be uncomfortable, painful, confusing, or challenging. We may wonder if God cares about us personally, given all the problems of the world today. When we are suffering, we may ask, "Where are you, God?" You may want to know and follow Jesus and yet feel as though your feet are stuck in cement boots. You may be feeling the sting of past injustices and question how God could possibly allow you to go through it. Your inner rage may be blocking your ability to surrender your heart to God. Perhaps you are willing to serve God but fear the places and people to whom God calls you.

God is not in the business of taking away our power through our surrender. For some, who at the hands of abusers have experienced power being taken from them, surrender may be a frightening proposition. Rather than taking away our power, it's quite the opposite; we are empowered to use our bodies, minds, and spirits rightly, justly, and lovingly in service to God, others, and ourselves. God gifts us with the power of light and love. We are encouraged to receive it and "regift" it to the world. Power that is abused is not of God but rather self-indulgent and evil. Some may say we surrender ourselves one day at a time. Some days it may be one hour at a time or one minute at a time. Let's even consider one breath at a time.

Take a moment and reflect on ways to focus on surrender in your daily experiences.

Surrender self-centeredness and place God at the center of your life. Exchange your wants for what God desires for you. Rather than continuing to fill yourself up with things you think will make you happy, you may find John Phillip Newell's words to be true: "God is found by subtraction not by addition." Completely empty yourself of yourself and be ready to experience the awesomeness of something much greater than you could ever imagine. It is amazing to discover what God has in store for you.

Surrender your expectations and instead look for the gifts hidden in the very ordinary experiences of your day. Expect miracles, not the ones of your making, but of God's. Dream outside the box! God doesn't live or work in a box, so be ready to find the Divine in unexpected places.

Surrender your tomorrows and choose to live in the now-ness of life. Keep yourself firmly planted in the present moment. Don't be in such a rush. Everything is revealed in its own time, so your trying to move ahead may prove to be rather frustrating and fruitless.

Surrender everything you think you know and open yourself to learning new things. It's perfectly all right to have opinions but limit your need to constantly share them without being asked. You'll experience a more contented heart when you don't need to have the last word. That always belongs to God.

Surrender the hard edges in exchange for a tender heart. Allow God to help you be with the uncomfortable. God will bless you with mercy, justice, tolerance, compassion, and the ability to forgive.

Surrender darkness and let God make you a beam of light for the entire world to see. Bring hope to those in need. Let God decide who is in need of your beams of light. God may choose your household, your community, or your church. Or you may be sent far from home. We all have unique itineraries from God. No need to compare your light to others; just concentrate on letting yours shine.

Rather than resolutions and promises, resistance and rigid control, and trying harder and harder, surrender your will to God and watch in amazement as God does for you what you've been unable to do yourself.

PERSONAL REFLECTION

Describe what surrender means for you at this time in your life?

What needs to be surrendered in order to move forward in your life?

If you were to "regift" to others that which God has given to you, what gifts would you be giving away?

What questions, thoughts, reflections arise in you at this time?

Chapter 3

Prayer

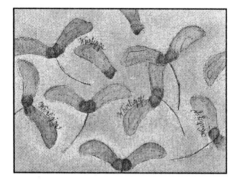

"In praying our experiences, we gather fragments of our life to become aware of who we are...our prayer is founded on the willingness and simplicity of being present to God in the unfolding of our story in honesty."
Joseph F. Schmidt, FSC

As a newborn baby, my parents brought me from the hospital to a three-family home owned by my grandparents. My Babci and Dziadziu (grandmother and grandfather), Polish immigrants, lived on the first floor, an uncle and aunt rented the second floor, and the third floor was reserved for family members starting out in married life.

My mother recalls that even before I could walk, I would crawl backwards down three flights of stairs and bang on the kitchen door searching out my grandfather. He would scoop me up into his arms and hug me with all his strength. The only vehicle he owned was a black Columbia bicycle. When I was a toddler, he would set me in his bike basket and take me for rides around the neighborhood. I easily bonded with this gentle man with a giant and humble heart.

After three years, we moved into a new home only two blocks away from my grandfather. As soon as I was old enough, I would walk or ride my bike to my grandfather's house and visit with him. We'd play games, rake leaves, or sit and visit on the front porch. Sunday mornings were set aside for Mass with my mother and Dziadziu. This routine continued through high school. As he was aging and needing assistance from a walker, I would help him navigate from the kitchen table to the front porch. He would sit in his chair and I took my spot on the top step. From there, we watched the daily goings on of neighbors and people passing by. Occasionally I'd chat about the weather or about something happening in school. All the while, he prayed silently and fingered the rosary beads that hung from his pants pocket.

I imagine God holding and caressing me in the womb of my mother and I hear the words of Isaiah, "I would not forget you! I have written your name on my hand." The first gift I received, even before I was gifted to my parents, was a promise of remembrance and love by God. A promise that he would give me the strength, the courage, and the wisdom to move through all of life's joys and storms with him. And, he would put people in my life to help guide me on the journey. I would not be alone. God is always answering prayer.

From conception, we are spiritual beings created to be holy. Prayer is our "always" opportunity to approach God with humility and ask that our character be molded and shaped by His will for us. Inside each of us there is a yearning for connection to our Creator. Sometimes we pay little attention to it. Sometimes we deny it. We may choose to ignore it and even fight it. If we chose to nurture that yearning, we find joy and contentment, truth and peace, and love and mystery beyond our wildest dreams. The more time we spend in prayer, the more our desire to dwell in God grows.

I believe it was my grandfather who planted seeds for me to better understand the importance of contemplative prayer; the ability to clear away outside distractions and concerns so that I may better hear and feel God's presence and guidance in my daily life. People take classes and attend programs to learn and practice this prayer form. For my Dziadziu, it all came naturally. He understood the benefits of prayer in the stillness.

The thing is, my grandfather spoke Polish and I spoke English. My Dziadziu taught me how to communicate through love and presence, not words. A touch, a smile, a visual cue, or laughter was all we needed to speak with one another. So, too, it is with God. We pray best when we are living into our life experiences and are aware of God's presence in them. No matter the form of prayer, our disposition or attitude, God listens and takes us just as we are.

We come to God via our connectedness to one another and the physical world around us. We cannot separate our prayer lives from our life experiences. We pray out of our internal and external experiences. We want to in some way feel God's presence within and outside of us. A maturing prayer life trusts God's presence even during those times we don't necessarily feel it. Maturing prayer is persistent and never gives up. It was Jesus who said, "Keep on asking, and you will be given what you ask for. Keep on looking, and you will find. Keep on knocking, and the door will be opened. For everyone who seeks, finds. And the door is opened to everyone who knocks."

Our immature ears may only hear, "…and you will be given what you ask for…" We have to remember this is God's timetable, not ours. We won't always get what we desire, right on the spot. We will always have God's love, presence, and comfort. Sometimes we learn our way into God's answers. At other times during life's journey, our hearts, minds, and desires are changed and we become in sync with God's plan for us.

We often feel inadequate when it comes to our prayer lives. We may wonder if God personally cares about our small concerns when there are so many huge problems in the world. God does care.

You may be suffering a loss, or grieving, and wonder where God is in all of those feelings. God is present.

You may be angry at past injustices and question how a loving God would allow you to go through that pain. God cried with you. God understands the inner rage that is presently blocking your heart.

You may want to serve God but fear the places to which you may be called and the people to whom you are called to serve. God will take away your fear and open your heart.

You may feel your life is so busy, you don't have time to pray. If you are that busy, you may need time to pray. God wants your attention.

Many people focus on the "doing" of prayer. Actually, we want to strive to *be* in prayer, in communion with the Divine. When we become consciously aware of God's presence in the very ordinary tasks and experiences of our days, we are praying into our experiences. Our prayer, then, is not only connected to what we may be doing, but who we are becoming, who God is calling us to be.

Saint Ignatius emphasized that our life's purpose is to praise, reverence, and serve God. In our daily activities and rest, we can periodically stop and simply pray with a simple question: "Am I praising, reverencing, and serving God by my words and actions this day?" If not, what changes can I make? If the answer is yes, then I express my thanks for the opportunities presented to me.

There are many forms of prayer: prayers of blessing, praise, and thanksgiving. We recite devotional prayers and ask for our petitions to be heard. We pray alone, in groups, in prayer services, and liturgy. We hold rosary beads, walk labyrinths, and form prayer circles. We pray ecumenically, we reflect on scripture, use centering prayer and lectio divina (Divine reading), singing songs, and even dancing in prayer. We may use words or allow the stillness to guide us into a more contemplative prayer life.

If you want to improve your prayer life, simply begin talking with God. If you really, really want to improve your prayer life, start listening to God! There are no rules for a fruitful prayer life, but there may be some things to notice as you continue to practice your conscious connection with God.

Be mindful of God's timetable. The problem with asking for specific things is that when they don't happen exactly as we planned, we become disappointed or angry with God. We may begin to think God doesn't care about us. In reality, God wants every great and good thing for us.

However, sometimes through no fault of our own, life interferes. People with bad intentions may attempt to rob us of life's goodness. Sometimes, because we are free to make our own choices, we reject God's plans in favor of our own. Evil forces are cunning and tempt us to focus on worldly treasures rather than spiritual treasures. We cannot understand why some people's crosses seem so heavy compared to our own. The answers as to why God allows suffering never feel sufficient.

Often times, when we seem to have more questions than answers, prayer is a very powerful and energizing way to express our doubts, confusion, or unrest with God. Whether private or communal, liturgical or devotional, expressed in words or in the silence of our heart, prayer is our connection to the Beloved. God's timing is perfect. We may not always understand it. Prayer helps us to trust it.

Talk to God as if you are talking to a friend. Share your feelings, frustrations, sorrows, and joys. We don't have to wait for our hearts to change in order for God to receive our prayers. Don't be afraid to speak from the open wounds deep inside of you. Pray from your present experience. Whether thankful, joyful, or from a place of brokenness, God takes us right where we are.

Be flexible. They say if you want to make God laugh, share your plans with him. Our bucket list may be chock full of a whole lot of nonsense. And, by nonsense, I mean a lot of things that drag us down, create emotional havoc, and more work for ourselves than is necessary. Through prayer, we learn to let God help us prioritize what is important and what we can let go of. Sometimes the answer to prayer is "Yes," sometimes, "Not now," and sometimes, "No, I have a better plan," but there is always an answer, whether or not we recognize it. Remain flexible because God may have something more fabulous in store for you than you could ever dream.

Bring your worries to God. The worries that incapacitate you, hold you back, and keep you in fear—turn them over to God. Let go and let God do the work. Letting go doesn't mean giving up. It means you trust God with your insights, gut instincts, and intuitions. How will you know God is in charge? You will feel free of worry because you trust God to give you what you need to deal with all of life's circumstances.

Seize moments of solitude and quiet. Breathe deeply and say, "God, let me see and feel you more clearly." A walk can be an opportunity to spend time with God. Just sitting in the silence of nature on a lunch break provides an opportunity to reflect on the graces and goodness in our lives. Begin with five minutes of silence each day. Gently push out distractions and let God fill the space with peaceful thoughts or images.

Pray from gratitude each day. Pay attention to the people who entered your day. What did they teach you? What did you offer them? Notice what delighted you. What gifts were revealed to you? What tickled your senses? Where did God show up today? Take note: is your prayer request list longer than your gratitude list?

At any point in your day, you can stop and notice what you've been doing, how you are doing it, who has helped you, how you got the supplies you needed, where they came from and whose hands may have made them. We have so much to be grateful for and very often it becomes so routine and rote to us that we hardly notice the gift in it. Pay attention to the gifts hidden in plain sight. They can come when we least expect them. They may arrive as the result of a difficult experience.

The author William Blake says, "We are put on earth a little space...that we might learn to bear beams of love." We bear beams of love through living into our prayer experiences. We will find holiness and wholeness rather than perfection. We will see the gift we are to others as well as the gifts we receive from others. Filled with the Spirit, we will be moved intuitively to serve God and others. As we surrender our fears and open ourselves to a God of Possibilities and Surprises, we will feel hopeful. We learn to trust that God can do for us what we cannot do alone. Inner peace and contentment grows as we find time for rest and renewal. A serious nature is gently opened to gifts of laughter, joy, and a sense of humor.

Pray. Ask. Pray. Receive. Pray. Give. Pray. Let your day begin and end in prayer.

PERSONAL REFLECTION

Describe your ideas about prayer. Has your prayer life changed over the years? How so?

Recall a moment in time when you have prayed into your experiences. How does it feel to have those memories come into your consciousness?

Have you experienced a gift hidden within a cross you've carried? Explain.

Write a simple prayer about your experiences this day.

What questions, thoughts, or reflections arise in you at this time?

Chapter 4

Trust

"And the day came when the risk to remain tight in the bud was more painful than the risk it took to blossom."
Anais Nin

Sister Florence was a teacher, friend, spiritual advisor and mentor, not only to me, but also to so many others. When she died unexpectedly during the Thanksgiving break, it left me feeling numb for a while. The School of Spirituality lost one of its finest educators. She was a faith-filled woman, full of wisdom and willing to share her gifts unselfishly. Her simplicity and grace were qualities I admired. Rather than advice, Florence often would ask a question that helped a person go deeper inside to find the answers. She was the consummate spiritual director. I felt the loss but also the appreciation of having been touched by this wonderful woman's spirit.

As days passed, I prepared for the Christmas season and Florence was very much in my thoughts. On Christmas Eve morning, while my husband and boys were still asleep, I slid out of bed into the darkness and began my morning ritual. With eyes half open, I layered my clothing and prepared for my jog through town. As I began to climb and then descend out of my winding driveway, I was distracted by so many thoughts and questions regarding my work. I had been contemplating leaving my job at the end of the school year. I was still in the throws of weighing the pros and cons and my morning jogs allowed me time to *pray and discern God's direction. It seemed that for months I had been contemplating my next move in life, and I was feeling a bit scared. Leaving my job meant giving up the steady paycheck I'd grown accustomed to, the titles that I clung to, and work that structured my days. Most importantly, I would be leaving a place and people I'd grown to love. On the other hand, resignation would free me up to explore new options and opportunities, although I had no idea what those might be. My job left little time for me to explore personal dreams and desires. Without driving myself crazy, I was trying to pay attention to the voice of the Spirit that seemed to be tugging at me. Resigning my position as campus minister meant taking a leap of faith. I described the feeling as jumping off a cliff with a parachute on my back. I was in charge of the preparations and God was in charge of the timing and the landing. I wasn't necessarily promised a smooth ride; however, the instructions were simple enough: "Trust Me."*

As I jogged, I recall looking up at the dark and cloudless sky, and I began this conversation in my head with Sister Florence. "What should I do, Florence?" I asked, with confidence that my heavenly angel was listening. I assured her I needed her guidance on this one. As I debated the pros and cons in my head, snow crunched beneath my feet, and ever so quietly I heard her response in the form of a question. "What is your heart telling you, Kathy?" Florence would never tell us what to do but rather encourage us to explore the answer that comes from the Spirit. Her trust in God assured me that I, too, would muster the courage to do the same.

The morning was still very dark, yet crystal clear and chilly. It was very still with little wind. I began to walk up my driveway, and at the top of the hilly drive, suddenly stopped, awed by the sight of a gazillion stars in the sky. The snow on the trees looked like a thousand glimmering spider webs suspended in air against the morning sky. At that moment, I felt an intense peace and joy within me. My shoulders relaxed. My mind drifted. I breathed slowly. I couldn't help myself. I needed to take it all in. I lay out on the driveway, arms outstretched and legs extended, just looking to heaven and breathing in the sight before me. I felt an energy pulsing inside me. Right then and there I felt the presence of a most delightful Spirit. Deep within were the words I'd heard Florence repeat in class: "there is only a one letter difference between play and pray. God has heard your many prayers. It's time to relax and to play." I had been praying patiently and waiting for God's answer.

The pristine snow was inviting me to experience being a child once again. I decided to make snow angels outside every window of the house so that when my family got up in the morning an angel would be waiting for them. I lay outside my kitchen window and moved my arms from my sides toward my head making wings. Then I pushed the snow with my legs forming the angel's skirt. I felt the angel's form gently caressing my body. I continued to tromp through the almost waist-high snow to the pool deck, then outside the living room. I made my way around the house and created angels in front of each bedroom window. After the last angel was completed, I lie there watching the dark morning welcome the first light of the day. The stars were disappearing and softly I spoke to Florence, "my earth angels want my heaven's angel to know I miss you dearly, but I feel your presence." As I got up and shook off the snow, I breathed in an air of gratitude and looked once more at the early morning sky before heading into the house for a warm shower and some tea.

Later that day, I took a picture of the snow angels I had created in the early morning hours. Several thoughts went through my mind as I stared at the pictures. This very ordinary experience brought such joy. I thought about how many times in the past I denied myself these moments because I told myself I was too busy for this "nonsense." This particular day I trusted my heart and allowed the Spirit to move me in a playful and prayerful way. In a sense, I was lost in God, completely trusting that the answers were within me.

It was then, in a moment of quiet prayer, that I made my decision. I was going to take a leap of faith and make the changes necessary in my work life. I would trust my inner urgings and allow the Spirit to lead the way. God would provide earth angels as well as heavens' angels to guide my way. I knew that while it probably would not be easy, it was simple, as simple as a beautiful angel created in the snow with love.

Trust begins with the admission that we cannot handle all of life's questions, concerns, and circumstances alone. By acknowledging our need for God we open ourselves up to the strength and wisdom that comes not through logic alone, but rather by intuition and faith. By placing our trust in God we completely free ourselves from worry. We feel in harmony with the universe. We welcome the people who gift us with their wisdom. The question of, "what's next?" is replaced by, "what's happening right now?" We abandon all needless distractions. We live in the moment, willing to accept it, move with it and through it, knowing God is there to shine a light into it.

Sometimes we can become so focused on controlling one thing we forget to trust that God has the big picture covered. Other times, we're looking so far ahead or behind us, that we forget to pay attention to what is right in front of us. In order to remain focused on God's will for us we need to remain in close conscious contact with God. Prayer and meditation help us to do that.

We place our desires, thoughts, words, and deeds in God's hands. Once we've placed ourselves in God's care, we let go of our need to control anything. We pay attention to our gut instincts and trust that God is present in them. We listen to the quiet voice within that gives us direction. As God works through others, we are grateful for the gifts they present to us. We do this free of worry, judgment, and fear. The act of turning our thoughts and actions over to God is one of faith. In doing so, we are free to choose a path.

The world has a way of pulling us this way and that. We can be enticed by external things that are bigger, better, faster, and stronger. Through our own choices or by circumstances, we are faced with evil and joy, war and peace, injustice and justice. Trusting God's plan means we are willing to enter into and accept the reality of the present moment. We may not like it, but we accept life on life's terms, knowing God is present to help us through it. We also trust that God's presence in others will be shown to us.

It's difficult to trust when life feels overwhelming. By letting go of the illusion that we are in control of our lives, we begin to notice that our choices open up exponentially. It's one of life's spiritual paradoxes. God does not interfere with life. God does not change events. God is present with us in every aspect of our lives. Therefore, we enter into the Mystery of God through faith. We trust God to guide us because of faith, not because of what we see.

It's not easy to live in the "not-knowing." These are the times we find comfort in those who share words of hope and wisdom. We look to spiritual ancestors for their insights. We pray for the Holy Spirit to provide whatever it is we need to move through the experiences and circumstances of our day.

We often hear the phrase, "we need to let God do the footwork." A wise mentor once suggested we put God in charge of our feet! God can handle it all.

PERSONAL REFLECTION

The not knowing that comes with change can be difficult. Describe how trust or the lack of trust has influenced changes in your life.

What is it that holds you back from growing into the person God is calling you to be? What do you need to let go of? Whom may you need to let go of? Do you trust God's presence in your experiences?

Who are the people you trust to help you in your life? What is it that makes them trustworthy?

What questions, thoughts or reflections arise in you at this time?

Chapter 5

Balance

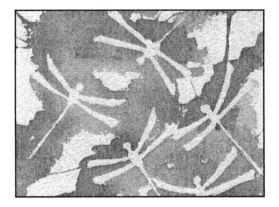

*"Happiness is not a matter of intensity
but of balance, order, rhythm and harmony."*
Thomas Merton

During the time in my life when I was struggling with an eating disorder, I felt a physical, emotional, and spiritual imbalance. It is impossible to remain attached to any substance, person, place, or idea, and feel completely at peace. When my every waking thought was about what I was going to eat or how I was going to stop myself from eating, there was no inner peace. It's as if a battle was raging inside of me. My body was craving food in order to calm the obsession, to fill a void, or push down emotions. My brain was passing along mixed messages such as, "a little bit won't hurt" or "you'll regret this later." I was torn by the compulsion and what I knew to be the truth.

My normal rhythm was completely turned on its heels. Fear and worry began to rob me of joy. I found myself trying to please others, afraid they would not accept me otherwise. I began to avoid social activities and isolated myself from others. The shame and guilt were overwhelming. There was an enormous amount of self-judgment, and therefore I expected judgment from others. I was envious of the peace and joy others seemed to have in their lives and wanted it more consistently for myself.

Often, my anger and frustration were directed toward those I trusted, family members and friends. If I couldn't do things perfectly, I decided not to do them at all. Taking a risk was out of the question if I thought there was a chance of failure.

I became impatient, often living in the past or anxious about the future. My prayers focused on my own desires rather than on accepting God's plan for my life. I often asked for answers and rarely listened for a response. My knuckles were bloody from banging on heaven's door. I felt as though God could not be bothered by my insignificant requests. Furthermore, because I could not control my compulsive eating behaviors, I didn't expect God to care about me. Why should God care if I had given up? I frequently held pity-parties at my own expense.

Functioning well in my work, home, and social life, didn't necessarily mean I was managing them very well. My life may have been somewhat efficient, but my capacity to really live life to the fullest was diminished spiritually, emotionally, and physically. My life was out of balance and I desperately sought out opportunities to restore or realign it.

Balance is an inside job. It's feeling at peace even when chaos is swirling all around us. Balance is being connected with God, others, ourselves, and the natural world in such a way that no matter what is happening, we have a choice about how we will react to outside stimuli. It is being present in the now of life, confident that all we need, God can provide for us.

There are probably a million books, tapes, websites and DVDs dedicated to helping us lead more balanced lives. We are bombarded with commercials for diet and weight loss programs that promise us a balanced, healthy weight, companies that hire consultants to help their employees balance work and home responsibilities, exercise routines that focus on our core, yoga poses to help us maintain our equilibrium, financial experts who warn us about balancing our checkbooks, clothing consultants to help us balance our "look," and consultants to help us organize our closets.

So, why, then, are so many people out of rhythm? Could it be that we are either over-stimulated or so tired running from one activity to another that we're not familiar with what it feels like to maintain a sense of balance in our lives? Is it possible that we are searching for answers outside ourselves?

Many people are experiencing life at the extremes. We are either working or playing at fever pitch or practically wiped out on the couch at home. Little things can send us into a tizzy, while important things are too overwhelming and therefore ignored.

We often find ourselves trying to derive our happiness from the things of this world. If our life is feeling out of rhythm, it may be time to redirect our thoughts and prayers toward God. Then allow God to energize us as he sees fit. We are receiving messages everyday about what we need to remain balanced. The problem could be we aren't listening or setting our priorities in the right order.

We surely cannot go through this life in perfect balance all of the time. But, to remain in a state of imbalance causes physical, emotional, and spiritual illness. We are striving for wholeness, toward restoration and fitness in all areas of our life.

Imagine a three-legged stool. One leg represents your physical life, one leg your emotional life, and the third leg your spiritual life. In order to balance comfortably on the stool, each leg must be in proportion to one another. Balance is necessary regardless of age and gender. Children as well as adults need time to play, to work, to create, to rest, to renew their bodies and spirits, and to allow time to discover new opportunities. When we neglect to exercise our bodies we may feel sluggish. If we are worrying over something that is happening a month from now, our energy may diminish in the present. If we fail to take time for quiet reflection, our minds and souls feel depleted.

I encourage you to begin finding ways to bring balance into your life without judgment. Today, take the time to do one thing that helps keep each leg of your stool balanced.

- Pamper yourself. (If you only take five minutes, that works). Lie on a blanket under a tree, take a bath, light a candle, and sit quietly. Take time to stop "doing" and just let yourself be still. If, on the other hand, you are finding the couch becoming too comfortable for hours at a time, take five minutes to walk, stretch, turn off the TV, and simply move your body.

- Write down an important goal, dream, or desire. Pray with it and then send it out into the universe and let it go. Repeat this action every day. Simply notice what happens over time as you consciously allow your dreams and desires to be expressed.

- Take time to organize one space or niche in your life that needs it. Perhaps you can come up with a list of things you can let go of that have been taking up space physically, spiritually, or emotionally.

- Do one positive action for another person in complete anonymity.

- Accept a compliment. Give a compliment.

- Expect something wonderful to happen in your day. Find delight in something ordinary.

- Say one prayer every day, even if it is only "Thank You, God."

- Take a few minutes in silence to reflect on one gift you received in this day. Look deeper. Was the gift a lesson, an opportunity, words of wisdom or an insight?

- Spend some time outdoors. Take a walk around the neighborhood. Dress appropriately so that your body feels comfortable. Explore someplace new. Can you experience God in your surroundings?

- Take a deep breath in response to any stressors. Repeat this action a few times before making a choice to act or respond.

We cannot "have it all" but we can begin to notice those things that appear out of balance in our daily experiences. Our lives cannot be all work and no play or conversely, all play and no work. If you find your life becoming all about efficiency, learn to add some wonder and creativity. If your life seems to be drifting and rudderless, perhaps you need direction and support. If your life seems to be lacking the fire of the Spirit, maybe it's time to seek that out.

Balance is not about perfection. It is about inner peace and harmony. When our insides begin to feel a little twisted, we need to pay attention to "the something" that may help to untwist it. One small action may go a long way toward restoring balance in your life today.

PERSONAL REFLECTION

How proportional are the physical, emotional, and spiritual legs of your stool? Is there a leg or two that appears out of balance with the others?

Describe the positive and negative aspects of your physical, emotional, and spiritual life? Where do you see strengths and weaknesses?

Do you believe it's possible to live a more balanced life? Describe what a balanced life might look like to you. What small changes can you make right now to help you achieve more balance? What is the one thing you can start or stop doing tomorrow that will help you feel more balanced?

What questions, thoughts, reflections arise in you at this time?

Chapter 6

Perseverance

"Perseverance is not a long race;
it is many short races one after another."
Walter Elliot

One day while heading out to the track for practice, I took my usual path toward the field by crossing the student parking lot directly in front of the entrance to the school gymnasium. It was a beautiful sunny day and all was right with the world. I stopped short and could hardly believe my eyes as I neared the entrance to the first field where softball players were gathering for their practice. In huge white letters scrawled across the blacktop was my full name followed by the word "sucks". In those days, that word was not thrown around quite as easily as it seems to be today. The impact of seeing those words stung my heart deeply. My immediate feeling was one of embarrassment. I knew everyone coming out for practice would see this graffiti. There was nothing I could do but absorb the blow to my heart and my ego. I was crushed and didn't understand the cruelty of the person or persons who wrote it. I began to question myself and wonder if I had said or done something to offend or hurt anyone which would cause a retaliation of this sort, but came up empty.

With practice ready to begin, I headed to the track. Tears kept welling up in my eyes as I thought about the graffiti on the parking lot, but I could do nothing about it during practice. After a couple of hours of practice, the team began to disperse and walked back toward the locker rooms in small groups. I wanted to be alone. I saw people pointing out the graffiti to others while some quietly noticed and walked on. I'm not sure which made me feel worse, but it made no difference. Everyone saw it. I walked across the scribbled insult and pushed down every last bit of raw emotion into the deep recesses of my body somewhere. Truth be told, a part of me wanted revenge. Hurt and anger were now doing a tango together in the pit of my being.

I remember taking the late bus home from school that day. I felt as though I was the butt of some cruel joke that everyone but me was privy to. No one spoke to me during the entire bus ride, and just as well, because I was one word away from a total meltdown. It would not have been pretty.

I didn't want to tell my parents what had happened, somehow believing at the time that I was protecting them from the insult. During dinner, my sisters vented their anger about the situation, and it was "on the table" so to speak. They talked about returning to the school that evening with black spray paint to cover up the graffiti. Still smarting from the insensitivity of the deed, I remember feeling comforted by my sisters' feisty support. It somewhat broke up the heavy mood at the table. My parents tried their best to bolster me up with words of encouragement. All I heard at the time was blah, blah, blah! As my sisters continued to plot revenge, I found solace in my room. Although my heart was aching, the words my parents spoke to me took hold. I heard and felt the words as if an antacid were poured over my heart: "take the high road". Returning to the living room, I told my sisters to leave the graffiti as it was. They seemed flustered and didn't quite understand my response, but respected my wishes nonetheless.

The decision was made and my heart felt some lightness. I was going to walk over that graffiti every day to prove to myself (and I guess others) that those words would not define me. I was determined to do the right thing. There was a part of me that wanted the person or persons who wrote the remark to see that I would not stay beaten down under the weight of those words. I was willing to take that graffiti on as a badge of courage. While I definitely believe words hurt, I absolutely did not want them to define who I was.

The graffiti remained for at least a couple of weeks. I'm sure someone on the maintenance staff eventually took a black can of paint to the blacktop. To this day, on the occasion that I go up to the high school in my hometown to watch my nephew play basketball or to attend some event, as I enter that parking lot there is some memory of that incident that plays in my mind. The memory I'm left with is that of a young girl, probably a little naive about the world, who took a step toward seeing herself as God sees her, not as another person decided to define her.

My self-esteem was shaky, as it is with a lot of teenagers. I was quite sure of whom I was not, yet not quite sure of whom I was. Maybe someone did not like me; God forbid! Maybe someone did not like who he or she was and took it out on me. In the scope of life, the parking lot graffiti was a blip on the radar screen; however, lessons were taken from that rather ordinary high school experience.

While my recovery from food addiction has taught me a lot about persevering through difficult circumstances, it was this high school experience that resonated within me as I pondered moving forward in the face of difficulty. The point is, we've all experienced the unpleasantness of feeling kicked to the curb over the course of our lives. Those experiences have taught us valuable lessons about perseverance. Life, as we know from experience, isn't always going to be fair. People's reactions will not always be kind. We don't have to navigate difficulties alone. God places people in our lives to love and support us through the rough patches.

In every situation, God gifts us with opportunities to learn more about ourselves. Some people will persevere through great trials, but for most of us, it's about moving through a rough patch, followed sometime later by another rough patch, and so it goes. In the face of adversity, we learn to place others and ourselves in God's care.

In scripture, Timothy and Paul were good friends. During difficult circumstances, they stood side by side. Timothy, despite his own youthful struggles with self- esteem, encouraged and supported Paul in his ministry. God calls each of us, despite difficult circumstances, to stand by one another and persevere in the face of unfairness, injustice, and unkindness.

How do we persevere when we come face to face with small and big trials in our lives?

We can acknowledge the reality of the situation, even accepting there may not be much we can do about it. Look at difficult situations as opportunities to learn something new that can help you as you journey further in your life.

Talk things out with a person you trust. Sometimes just getting it out in the open decreases the power and lifts the weight it causes on your heart and mind. Surround yourself with people whose morals and values shine positively in the world. Stand firm in your values.

Instead of reacting while emotions are jumbled, just be with the situation, allowing yourself time to think more clearly. Once the highly charged emotions settle a bit, our minds begin to formulate more positive responses to help us cope.

Pray and seek guidance from God regarding the best actions to take, if any. Recognize that retaliation will more than likely be only a temporary fix and will probably eat away at you for a long time. God always helps us take the high road.

Find something in yourself that brings you joy. Keep a larger focus. Anything that is valuable or has value takes effort on your part. Find happiness in the small things. Use humor as a way to ease the intensity of a difficult situation or challenge.

Allow yourself to fail. Move past rejection. Keep your eyes peeled for new doors to be opened.

It's been a very long time since the graffiti experience. There is no bitterness or resentment; it is one of those things that I just have never forgotten. Perhaps, because of my work with adolescents, this particular story stayed with me. There is probably a similar story in each one of us, and a part of us that empathizes when a child shares with us the pain of embarrassment, rejection, loneliness, bullying, and the like. What we can share with them is a personal story about perseverance, how a little good, old-fashioned gumption can get us through what seems like an end-of-the-world crisis.

Stories of perseverance can encourage children and teenagers to see their worth. It's important to share with them that it's not necessarily how others see them, rather, how God sees them, that's truly important. Despite any difficulties or discouraging circumstances, they can be sustained by God's grace.

PERSONAL REFLECTION

Recall a significant moment in your life in which you persevered through a difficult situation. Describe the steps that helped you to get through it?

During a difficult experience, was there a time you were able to shift from negative feelings to those that were affirming? Recall the catalyst of that movement.

Describe an experience in which you believe others may have seen you differently than God sees you. How did it make you feel? What did you learn about yourself?

What questions, thoughts, or reflections arise in you at this time?

Chapter 7

Humility

*"It is impossible to begin to learn
that which one thinks one already knows."*
Epictetus

My desk phone rang at work and the voice at the other end was unfamiliar to me. The woman explained that she worked in a group home for those with mental illness. She asked if I would be interested in facilitating a group focused on spiritual recovery for those with eating disorders and food issues. To this day, I have no idea how she got my name or work number.

At the time, I had been praying for a community service opportunity to emerge. This opportunity was one hour a week. Better yet, it was only a couple miles down the road from the school at which I worked. It appeared to be a perfect opportunity.

At the first group meeting, there were about a dozen clients who seemed interested in returning each week. I was excited about all the possible things I could share with them. I collected books, prayers, stories, quotes...anything that would enhance the quality of the presentation and provide for interesting discussion.

After a couple months, interest in the meeting was clearly dwindling. Only a handful of people participated each week. I questioned myself over and over about how I could better engage the group. Some of the clients, because of side effects from their medication, had difficulty reading, while others read so painfully slow that the message was lost in translation. Still others would get up and walk out of the room because they had difficulty sitting still. Some shared on the topic and others were unable to follow the conversation. There were a few people who seemed engaged in the discussions, so I appreciated when they showed up for the meeting.

After several months, I began to question whether I could truly make a difference with this group of people. I was frustrated and confused and continually questioned God as to why I was there. Surely, I thought, there are places out there that could really use my gifts! I was on the brink of quitting when one day God spoke to me through raindrops.

It was the end of a tiring day at school. I didn't even notice that the skies had opened up and it was pouring outside. I just wanted go home and relax, but it was my weekly meeting day at the group home. I had no umbrella, so I ran to my car. Feeling soaked with rain and cold, I headed toward the group home. Because the parking lot at the group home was very small and a nightmare to negotiate, I always parked across the street. I sat in the car for a couple minutes hoping the rain would let up. When I realized that wasn't going to happen, I grabbed my book bag and purse, and made a dash for the corner.

As I was waiting for cars to clear before crossing the street, I noticed one of the gentlemen from my group waiting on the other side with an umbrella. He greeted me with a huge smile and hello. He told me he saw me coming and wanted to provide the umbrella so I wouldn't get rained on (too late for that!). It's what he said next that made the raindrops taste salty. With happiness in his voice, he looked into my wet eyes and exclaimed, "I'm so happy you came today, Kathy. We were waiting for you and thought the rain might keep you away."

God was speaking clearly to me. He was answering the question as to why I was there. You see, I thought I was there to pass along all my great wisdom and to share my experiences, strengths, and hopes with this group. I was going to help them through their difficulties and help them see the light with regard to how they use food in misguided ways. God's response: "Nope, not really what I intended." It appears my plans were much more complicated than God's simple plan.

I was called to this place to care about these people, not because of their abilities or disabilities. I was called to minister to them with love, care, and respect, to simply be present, to listen with my heart. They didn't care how much wisdom I had. They just cared that I showed up, and didn't forget them. For months, all the time and energy I had spent fretting over outcomes was unnecessary.

I left the meeting that afternoon with a clearer understanding of what God intended for me. I needed to just be me and to let them be them and together to do our best to provide "presence" for one another. With a sense of humor, God was able to show me the big picture: "It's not all about me!" It was a humbling experience. I learned that I have to put aside what I think I know or what I think is best in order to best serve God and others.

Humility is often misunderstood as belittling oneself. Becoming a "doormat" for someone is not true humility. To be humble is to love oneself as God loves. It is acknowledging the gifts that God has bestowed upon us and using those gifts to honor God in all our thoughts and actions. Therefore, there is no longer a need to take credit for our gifts but to thank the Divine for all he has bestowed upon us. We become smaller not in the sense of being unworthy of God's love, but rather to acknowledge the difference between the Creator and the created. A humble person also recognizes their shortcomings and is willing to ask God for help to remove them.

Humility

We live in a secular culture that often elevates and awards individual achievement and celebrity. We are encouraged to be the best at whatever we do. Promotions to the top are rewarded, and to win at all costs is often the expectation. There is nothing wrong with a desire to achieve a goal. However, we must ask ourselves, to whom does the credit belong? If we find ourselves swelling up with pride at personal achievement, perhaps we need a spiritual reminder of how we got there. A person growing in humility recognizes the signs of pride and makes a conscious decision to move away from feeding the self; instead, giving credit where credit is due. Everything we achieve comes as a gift from God.

There are simple steps we can take to move us toward a humble disposition:

- Be thankful for the gifts you receive from God. Do not hide them, but use them rightly and wisely as God calls you to do. Do not use your gifts for personal gain so much as to serve God and others in need of your gifts.

- Put aside what you think you know about God and let God surprise you! We can experience more by adopting an attitude that is always open and willing to learn.

- It's OK to say, "I don't know." We cannot solve all of our daily problems by ourselves. There is no need to pretend we have all the answers. Feel free to ask questions. Answers come on God's timetable, not our own. Be patient.

- Stop bragging! It's important that our thoughts and actions praise, honor, and serve God. Let others notice without bringing attention to yourself.

- Live in the present moment. Accept where it is you are in your life. You don't have to like it. But, like it or not, expect God to be present in it. You are not alone. God can help you move through any experiences or circumstances that life brings.

- Recognize your limitations and shortcomings. Pray that God will provide whatever you need to overcome your limitations. Ask God to remove your shortcomings. Then let God do it! For example, if you asked someone to wash your car, and then proceeded to get a bucket, sponge, and hose and washed the car yourself, your actions tell the person you think you can do it better. Adopt a true attitude of humility. Trust God to lead the way.

PERSONAL REFLECTION

What does the statement, "humility is accepting the difference between the Creator and created," mean to you?

Describe a humbling experience that helped you to grow closer to God.

What does it mean to you, to humble yourself before God?

What questions, thoughts, reflections arise in you at this time?

Chapter 8

Stillness

"This place inside of you is a place of silence, a place of utmost simplicity, as you breathe in and out with God. Know that you are always doing this breathing with God, and God is breathing with you... With whatever pain and struggle that are present in the world now or are yet to come, God's breath is always easy."
John Morton

Amidst some inner turmoil, someone once asked me to remember a time when I felt completely at peace. A time when my mind was still and my heart contented. It took me only a short moment to recall a small service job I had been given in eighth grade at my Catholic grammar school.

Once a month, usually on a Friday during the lunch period, I entered the sacristy of our huge church in order to clean all the brass candle followers (a brass socket with a lip that helped catch the wax drippings) from candles on the altar.

A few steps from the school playground and inside the backdoor of the church, our priest would set down a layer of protective plywood on a tabletop. Several candles were lumped together and lit. (I'm sure the fire marshal would have plenty to say about this practice today!) Taking a set of pliers, I picked up the brass followers one by one and held them in the flame until all the wax dripped off onto the plywood. Once the wax was melted, I placed the candle follower on another sheet of paper until all the followers were completed in the same process. After blowing out all the candles, phase two began. Taking a liquid brass cleaner, I would then clean and polish each brass follower. Finally, all would be gently placed back onto the altar candles or stored for future use.

During this process I could hear my classmates cavorting out on the playground and having fun. Despite missing recess with my friends, I remember looking forward with anticipation to this job because it was so quiet and peaceful. In retrospect, this simple task was a form of meditation. I was able to let go of all the stuff of my day and be present to this very simple task. I felt like I was in sacred space, in the presence of the Holy One. The process was familiar and repetitive; it was quiet, and I had a sense that this little service helped create a more beautiful church as well as create a wellspring of peace inside of me.

Think back to your childhood. Were there spaces you sought to be alone, perhaps to think or to not think so much or to talk things over with God? Chances are you didn't think of them as sacred spaces at the time. Sacred spaces are fluid and ever changing. They are places that allow us to be real, open, honest, and free.

Stillness is an inside job. Our body is the vessel through which we experience stillness. We come to God in this broken but delightful vessel and ask that it be filled with goodness, light, and love. We have the ability to create sacred space by quieting our minds and thinking of a place that feels safe and beautiful. Let your mind imagine such a space. Once you've created that space, you can return anytime you wish.

Stillness replenishes us; it allows our physical, emotional, and spiritual body to rest. Nothing is forced in stillness. Our mind is either free to wander or to gently focus on a particular thought. It is a space that God penetrates and negative energy dissipates.

When the world around us begins to fill up with distractions and chaos, it is useful to seek out our sacred space. During times of retreat, we may be alone, but not at all lonely. It is a time to withdraw from the stuff of life in order to rest in God's presence. Hiding out with God should become part of our daily routine.

Come as you are. If you are angry, settle yourself and see if God cannot help guide you through it. Hurt or lonely? Let God console you. Humorless? Allow God to soften your hard edges. No one seems to be listening? God will give you all the time you need to talk. Overwhelmed? Let God offer you a new perspective. Is trust difficult for you? Turn it all over to God who is used to handling even the most complicated issues. Has worry begun to paralyze you? Allow God to speak to your heart so you will be free to live without fear. Too busy? Spare five minutes and simply talk with God. Then listen in the stillness. Sick or tired? Come to the Healer for life-giving water.

Repetition often helps us to get into a healthy pattern of inviting God into the stillness. People have shared all kinds of experiences in which they encounter God in sacred spaces: resting under a tree, sitting or kneeling beside a flowing brook, climbing a mountain, bathing in a lake, walking in the rain, viewing an animal in the wild, or simply gazing at summer flowers in a garden. The experiences are as numerous as the stars in the heaven.

We spend a week every summer on a lake in the Adirondacks. One of my very favorite experiences is getting up before the sun rises and taking my kayak out on the lake. I paddle out to a quiet cove and remain still and just listen and feel what God is presenting to me. Not only do I feel my heart beating and my lungs filling and expelling air, I feel a connection to the vastness of the universe around me. All my senses are in tune with God's creations. One can only feel humbled in the "unquiet quiet" of nature.

An ordinary experience while on silent retreat became a powerful visual for me. I went to the chapel early in the morning and took a seat toward the back of the chapel. I began to pray by closing my eyes, relaxing my body, and asking God to fill the quiet inner space of my being. Initially, I felt the warmth and relaxation of the space. Soon thoughts began to creep in about a workshop I was going to be presenting later in the week. My mind began to wander and I felt myself being pulled away from the inner peace. Convinced I lost my ability to re-center, I opened my eyes and looked up at the cross. A smile came across my face and I thought to myself, "Jesus, you are here and present to me in this wonderful stillness and this is what I'm sharing with you...stuff...nothing I really need to concern myself with at the moment!" I went on, " since we have this time together, maybe I should tell you what is really on my mind and in my heart...the stuff that really matters today."

In that moment, I closed my eyes and had a visual of Jesus sitting beside me. I took in the feelings of having Jesus present with me. It was like having a friend beside me. I told him exactly what was in my heart. I felt at ease, relaxed, and willing to let go of all my anxieties and worries, all of which seemed self-perpetuated. He listened. He offered to unburden me. He encouraged me to visit often, wherever and whenever I chose.

It felt so real to me that it has been much easier to take time and sit with him more often. This was a heart thing, not a mind thing. The spaces in which I meet with Jesus, my friend, are varied: rocks, backyard chairs, by the pool. We even had an encounter at a baseball game! Not everyone will relate to God in a similar manner.
It may be that you experience God in a whisper, in silence, in movement or singing, a ritual, prayer, meditation, while exercising, or in nature. It all begins with a breath in the stillness. Asking God to quiet your body and mind so you may receive the Spirit that moves and dances in stillness.

Stillness is not entirely about location. While it is true for me that a quiet setting has its advantages, I find that ultimately stillness is about quieting the mind and finding that tranquil place inside of me where I am sure of God's presence. Heck, I've been able to experience that feeling in the checkout line at Target on a particularly busy holiday weekend!

Perhaps St. Francis de Sales in his short prayer conveys it best:

"Never be in a hurry; do everything quietly and in a calm spirit.
Do not lose your inward peace for anything whatsoever, even if your whole

world seems upset. Commend all to God, and then lie still and be at rest in His bosom."

PERSONAL REFLECTION

Describe your experiences of stillness.

What is it you need to bring to God in the stillness?

Recall sacred spaces of your past, of your present. What is your experience of stillness in these sacred spaces?

What questions, thoughts, reflections arise in you at this time?

Chapter 9

Honesty

" A wise person is hungry for truth, while the fool feeds on trash."
Proverbs 15:14

I've spent way too much time believing the lies: If you don't look a certain way, you won't matter. If you don't have certain things, you will not be happy. If you don't believe a certain way, you will be discounted. If you don't pray in accordance with a particular tradition, you will not be saved. Your description of God doesn't measure up. Spiritual pursuits are for the weak-minded. Dreams are just that; they rarely come true.

For years I've described a nasty entity that lives in my head and wants the opposite of every good thing I desire. Initially, I described the entity as internal beasts or dragons that seemed to rear their ugly heads when I was most vulnerable. Soon I gave this entity a name: the Itty Bitty Nitty Gritty Committee, the IBNGC, for short. Self-doubts, negative thinking, self-sabotage, and self-deception are among its most potent weapons. This committee takes every opportunity to twist and confuse my thoughts until I no longer feel like my authentic self. Truth becomes twisted and distorted by this committee of lying chameleons.

Let's look at a perfectly simple example of how cunning the IBNGC can be. Let's imagine something that is common in my work. I'm facilitating a program for a group of twenty women. My presentation seems to go well. Conversation seems to be flowing following my talk. The response from my audience appears warm. There is plenty of laughter and discussion, but I notice one person in the group doesn't seem to be responding no matter what is said or done.

The committee begins to speak. "How can you engage this person? You're not making a good impression. This person isn't impressed. What did you say that put her off?" The IBNGC is trying to convince me that for some reason I failed. Following the program, you'd think the committee would quiet down, but the drive home provides more head drama. "What could I have said or done to make an impression?"

The truth could be that this person had a difficult day and just wanted to listen, or was an introvert who internalized the message, but wasn't eager to share her thoughts. Or she may have been disappointed with the presentation. So what? The truth is, I can only do my best and leave the outcomes in God's hands. The committee wants to suck me into its web of feeling inadequate. The IBNGC wants total control. Under no circumstances does the committee want me to be grateful for being me.

Certainly, I have cheated, exaggerated my capabilities. I've gossiped about someone when I knew what I was saying was not true. I've lied to someone because I thought by telling the truth it might hurt his or her feelings. I've refused to see the other side of an argument because I thought my point of view mattered more. I've told little white lies and big, bold lies. I've rationalized, pretended, and worn several masks. That's the truth, and it's not pretty. However, I also possess many gifts that I second-guess or have difficulty accepting because I allow a committee in my head to play with the truth. This amazing vessel that God gifted to me has many cracks. Today, I work at accepting the truth whether it comes through joy or pain. Honesty leads me to freedom. I can become the person God intends for me to be.

We're challenged every day to make decisions with a sincere heart and mind. When we begin to look honestly into our hearts to see where we stand with God and others, we may be surprised with what we find.

Our little white lies, our inability to take responsibility for our own actions, and our self-deception only serve to build a wall between us and God, and us and others. We can look at our dishonesty in the form of lying, cheating, self-righteousness, and denial of our gifts and talents. When we talk the talk, but don't walk the walk, are we not being dishonest? Our dishonesty may show in our unwillingness to accept our present reality or by being too willing to pile blame upon another. Perhaps we don't trust our gut instincts despite our prayer to let go and give all to God. We may place our opinions above everyone else's, wanting to dominate the direction of conversation. We may rationalize something rather than pay attention to our conscience. Do we point out others' human failings while denying our own?

Honesty is the first step in getting things right with God and others. A mentor used to paraphrase John's words by saying, "the truth will set you free, but first it's going to tick you off!" Being honest about our feelings, our perceptions, or our realities absolutely changes things. Not having everything go your way may upset you a bit at first. Sometimes we want what we want even when it is not right or good for us. Spiritual maturity means being honest with ourselves, others and God. It means accepting what is in front of us at this moment in time and working through it, not denying it.

By looking honestly at ourselves, we move from a place of arrogance and self-importance to a place of self-respect and dignity. In twelve-step work, we understand this process as "taking inventory."

To better understand the concept of taking inventory, imagine you are managing a convenience store and the owner asks you to take inventory of what is on the shelves. You would write down exactly what appears on the shelves today, not a month ago. The point is we must examine our lives as they are today. If something in our past causes us to react or do something that damages others, our relationship with God, or ourselves, then we need to look honestly at it. However, we don't need to rehash the past and beat ourselves up if over time we have had an honest resolution to a problem or concern.

As we become more aware of how our actions have separated us from God and others, we have an opportunity to open up our hearts and minds to change. We don't set about trying to change ourselves. We ask God to make us willing to do and say those things that he intends for us. This takes practice and over time you will find a more authentic and honest person emerging.

Once you become willing to look honestly at yourself, there may be feelings of guilt, shame, or resentment that linger as a result of your new awareness. Talking with a trusted friend, mentor, therapist, or member of the clergy helps to free our minds and hearts in order to follow God's plan for us.

Catholics have been participating in the sacrament of Reconciliation for centuries. It is the face-to-face exchange between priest (God's representative in the flesh) and the person confessing, which brings about a healing experience beyond simply words. Meeting face-to-face with another human being in order to ask for forgiveness adds a component of humility. In reconciliation, we seek to express our sorrow by prayerfully examining and giving expression to our brokenness.

Becoming honest with ourselves takes some internal unearthing. Sharing what I find with God has always seemed pretty easy to me, since God isn't sharing any of our secrets with anyone. Sharing our shortcomings with another person takes humility and trust. Words cannot explain it. It is an experience of release and letting go that makes the heart and mind clearer. We reconcile not to make ourselves feel good, but to right a wrong; to ask God to make us aware of how not to repeat harmful actions. Usually this has the effect of making us feel clean and fresh inside; we have a new chance, a new beginning. We can do this as often as is necessary. It is important to allow our merciful God to change us as he sees fit. Sometimes our biggest battle is with ourselves. We want to change ourselves into what we think we're suppose to be, or to conform to what we think others expect of us. Allow God to do for you what you cannot do for yourself.

An honest self-assessment frees us up to witness small miracles along the way. Every time God is able to move us from fraudulence to realness, we experience spiritual growth. We are free to love others and God because we are learning to love the person God created us to be. Gone are the masks, the drama, the inflated ego, and the arrogance. Once again, this is about progress, not perfection.

A word of caution: in *our* zeal to be honest, we must always be careful that our honesty does not in any way cause intentional harm to another person. Opening old wounds that could tear people down is not our intention. We are taking care of *our* inner lives. That is, we are taking care of the stuff on our shelves and letting others take care of what's in stock on theirs.

There is a simple and effective way to take inventory. You may want to begin the process by taking each word in this book and writing your honest appraisal of where you shine and where you need more work with regard to each one. This exercise helps you to identify areas in your life that may need improvement or change. The rest is up to God. Just take it one step at a time.

I suggest you get a simple, wire-bound notebook from any dollar store. (Save your "pretty" journal for writing pretty things.) Writing honestly doesn't always look pretty. Be ready to tell it like it is. Sit once a day and start out slow, maybe give yourself five minutes of truthful writing on one word. Some days the words will flow, others not so much. It's the discipline of honestly searching your heart that is important.

Find a quiet space to write without being interrupted. As this is a discipline, some people find the use of a timer helpful. You may want to place the word *honesty,* for example, at the top of the page. Initially, it may be helpful to use the reflection questions found in this book or to write your own questions regarding the word *honesty* as a starting point. List examples of how you've exhibited honesty in your daily life. What role does honesty or the lack of honesty play in your relationships, daily activities, and faith life? What specific actions have caused positive or negative reactions in you or with others? Who has been affected by your actions?

Before you begin to write, pray. You don't have to say anything more than, "God, inspire my thoughts, and let me honor you and myself by being truthful." Remember to write both the shortcomings and the gifts you see in yourself. It's "what's on the shelf" right now.

After writing, spend a few moments in quiet. Let God speak directly to your heart. I promise you will find this to be a life-changing experience if you commit yourself to this process of honest evaluation. Keep in mind this is not a "beat-yourself-up" exercise or an "I've got to change myself" exercise. This is a "let God love me until I love me the same way" exercise.

PERSONAL REFLECTION

How has dishonesty hurt my relationship with God, others, and myself?

Describe an experience in which the truth has set you free?

How have you handled situations where your truth conflicts with that of an institution, the workplace, family, or friend?

What questions, thoughts, reflections arise in you at this time?

Chapter 10

Vulnerability

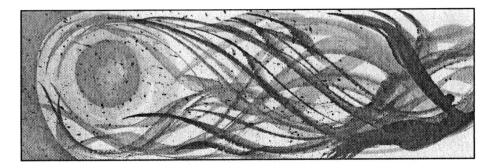

"When we were children, we used to think that when we were grown-up we would no longer be vulnerable. But to grow up is to accept vulnerability... To be alive is to be vulnerable."

Madeleine L'Engle

My patient approached me quietly in the hallway with his request. Would I be willing to escort him to a support meeting on the second floor of the hospital? Being a student nurse on the psychiatric unit, I needed permission from the head nurse. She assured me that it would be fine to attend the meeting with him.

When we arrived, the room was set up with a large meeting table in the center surrounded by soft, cushioned chairs. I chose a seat that was outside the circle and against the wall. No one questioned my being there, so I assumed, being in a nurses' uniform, this kind of thing occasionally happened. I watched as people entered the room and greeted one another with handshakes and hugs. They smiled and laughed with one another. Their appearances suggested they came from all walks of life.

As the meeting began, I was amazed at how vulnerable these people were with one another. Story after story was filled with joy, pain, loss, and hope. What wasn't lost on me was the fact that I was listening to bits and pieces of my own story being told by other people. They shared openly and honestly their shame, guilt, and the inability to stop their compulsive behavior on their own. Some talked about prayers that seemed to go unanswered, and yet there was such optimism that one day answers would come.

How was it that total strangers were brave enough to share their most intimate thoughts and feelings with one another? I thought to myself, "this takes guts!" I noticed the respect given to each person in the room; the time and the presence given to each person who shared. No one dismissed another's thoughts or feelings. They talked about a God of their understanding, each tolerant of the other's ideas. Despite the desperation and sadness in some of their stories, each remained hopeful.

As I walked my patient back to the psychiatric unit, I was lost in my own thoughts. I wondered to myself if meetings existed for people who, like me, overate. When I returned to my dorm that afternoon, I looked in the phonebook, and there it was, a recovery group for people who overeat. I attempted to dial the phone but I could not. Fear replaced resolve. I was afraid someone would know me (sick thinking). Instead I once again vowed to pull myself up by the boot-straps and take care of myself, by myself (more sick thinking). Surely, one did not need help to stop overeating. After all, "I should be able to lick this problem on my own," I thought. I went back to rigid methods, trying to control my weight on my own. God, however, had not abandoned me.

Looking back, I now see this chance encounter opened a door to new possibilities. Although I did not follow through immediately, I always remembered what I heard and how I felt as I sat at that table on the second floor of the hospital. There finally came a day when I agreed to get serious about my own recovery, and was willing to take a risk and ask for what I needed and desired.

It's like the story of the man in the flood. The waters around his home begin to slowly rise. The water is rising toward his front door and a policeman comes to warn him, but he waves him off, saying he wants to remain in his house. "God will answer my prayers," he calls out to the policeman. And the policeman shakes his head and moves on. The water continues to rise, and soon his furniture is floating in water that has risen up to his first floor windows. The Coast Guard comes by in a boat and tells the man it's time to leave. The man shouts back, "my trust is in God; he will answer my prayers and save me." After several hours, the water rises so high that the man must swim out of a second-floor window and onto the roof. A helicopter comes by and a rope is released to save the man, but he refuses. He is shouting at the top of his lungs, "God will answer my prayers and save me!" The floodwaters are raging, and the man is swept away and drowns. When he gets to heaven and he sees God, he asks him why he didn't answer his prayers and save his life. God responds, "I sent the policeman, the boat, and the helicopter. What more did you want?"

Sometimes it takes a while to recognize life-affirming messages being sent our way. Perhaps we're not willing or ready to accept and share our vulnerability with others. We may need to be convinced we are worthy of the help, love, and support of others. Fear often holds us back. It binds us up. When we are fearful, it's very difficult to ask for what we need or desire. There are times, too, that our coping skills— perhaps because of life's stressors—are weakened. We all can relate to experiences in our lives when we refuse to ask—or find it difficult to ask—for help, to our own detriment. Shame can hold us back from being vulnerable with others. "Am I good enough? Will you like and accept me if you know certain things about me?" We all experience these feelings to one degree or another.

Ultimately, my life was saved, physically, emotionally, and spiritually because of a group of men and women I never knew, and a man suffering in his own private hell that asked me to take him to a meeting. Coincidence? I think not. The Spirit was attempting to move me and did, in fact, do that. Looking back I'm able to see that because of my fears, I was not ready to invite God into the process consciously. However, God was present in my resistance. I never stopped praying that one day I would feel that same hope others experienced when they focus on their relationship with God.

Within the context of a safe relationship or relationships, we can reveal layers of our story to others. We too will appreciate people who are open and willing to remove masks and reveal their authentic selves to us. Getting beyond surface conversation and going deeper with someone who is willing to share his or her journey moves us in an empathetic way. The good, the bad, and the ugly are presented not with shame, but with recognition of true humanity. Yes, there is risk in revealing ourselves to others. However, what else is there if not for a desire to feel connected to others? That's what life is all about, our interconnectedness. When you discover a respectful, safe, and tolerant relationship in which you can be your authentic self, that is golden.

So the question becomes, how do we begin to view vulnerability as an asset rather than a liability?

- Recognize your resistance. It's difficult to share our strengths and shortcomings with others. Whether it is fear, shame, pride, or anything else that holds you back from being authentic, just acknowledge it.

- Risk sharing your hurts, joys, and dreams with someone you trust. You don't have to do this all at once. Connecting with others is a desire of the heart. Let your heart shine.

- Be courageous. How people receive us is not our business. If we are centered in God, our intentions are good. We can relax in the knowledge that they can take us as we are or not. It's their gain or loss. You no longer have to try to be someone you are not.

- Open yourself up to the possibilities. Learn how others get through difficulties, make dreams come true, build self-esteem, and find purpose in their lives.

- Trust in God when you are at your most vulnerable moments. God is with you there. God wants you to have a peaceful and contented heart. Listen. Share. Remain teachable. God wants to turn your resistance into joy.

- Show gratitude for breakthrough moments. Every time you remove a mask and risk becoming the person God intends for you to be, say, "Thank You."

PERSONAL REFLECTION

Identify times in your life when you've been vulnerable with another person or persons. How did it feel for you? What gifts did you receive in this encounter?

In what ways does being fully alive require you to be vulnerable?

What questions, thoughts, or reflections arise in you at this time?

Chapter 11

Humor

"A sense of humor...is needed armor.
Joy in one's heart and some laughter on one's lips is a sign
that the person down deep has a pretty good grasp of life."
Hugh Sidney

The children were lined up in the cafeteria of a Catholic elementary school for lunch.

At the head of a table was a large pile of apples. The nun made a note, and posted it on the apple tray, "Take only ONE! God is watching."

Moving further along the lunch line, at the other end of the table was a large pile of chocolate chip cookies.

A child had written a note, "Take all you want. God is watching the apples!"

Did you just smile? While I cannot prove this, it seems to me that since we're created in the image and likeness of God, and because God has a sense of humor, our sense of humor is buried deep in our DNA. We are born with joy in our heart and soul. Over the years, family, friends and — often — complete strangers may have nurtured it. A spiritual life devoid of humor is quite frankly, devoid of the Spirit.

Much of my life's work has centered on healing. Associated with healing, there is always an aspect of pain, whether physical, emotional, or spiritual. Yet, there is nothing so cleansing and refreshing as a humorous moment to lighten a load. I thank God every day for the comedians among us, those who make us belly laugh or bring a simple smile to our face. All the medicine in the world cannot do what simple joy and laughter can do for healing those who are ill.

When I can laugh at myself, it is undoubtedly the height of being well. Caregivers understand that in order to continue giving joy to others, we must posses it within ourselves. An empty well cannot quench the thirst of those in need.

God plays and laughs with us on a daily basis. Sometimes it happens when we're self-assured, thinking we have all the answers. Life will throw us a curveball just to remind us of who's in charge. Or, when we're taking ourselves way too seriously, the right person comes along to help you laugh at yourself. Whimsical moments happen all the time. Have you ever driven down the highway, lost in your thoughts, and decided to crank up the car radio, only to get carried away in the music? You don't notice the car beside you until it has almost passed. The occupants, obviously amused by your solo karaoke of *Brown-Eyed Girl*, roar with laughter. We've all had moments when we're caught off guard and have to chuckle at ourselves.

A sense of humor helps us to break the ice in tense situations. Soulful humor often rescues us from the doldrums and is a spiritual experience. When shared with others, it connects us to God in sacred joyfulness.

Laughter and joy are cathartic for our souls. Our bodies respond physically to humor in such a way that we actually feel better about others and ourselves.

God wants more than anything for us to feel joyful. There's something sacred about silliness that touches deep within us. Life has enough serious and painful moments; sometimes it may feel like one struggle after another. A sense of humor goes a long way toward giving us some relief and a new perspective.

Think back to your childhood memories. Who made you laugh? Things that may not have seemed funny at the time may have you rolling in laughter as you reminisce.

As kids we'd sit around the supper table and inevitably one of us would spill our milk. My usually mild-mannered dad just had little patience for it and would start his rant: "can't we get through one meal without spilling something?" or "you've got to be kidding me—again?" or sometimes a profanity might slip his tongue. Watching him making such a big deal over the spilt milk just sent my mom into a fit of laughter, and she would leave the table, not wanting to further infuriate my dad! Eventually she'd return, make a comment toward my dad, and then he'd crack a smile and all was well. She was capable of tempering my dad's flare-ups and making us smile at the same time.

It was the same with the family Christmas tree. My father seemed to tangle with the tree every year and somehow turn it into an unintended comedy. With seven excited children wanting to help pick out the tree and get it up as soon as possible, there were tense moments. He had to fit the tree in the stand, untangle lights, find the one damaged light that caused half the string to go dead, step out of the way of ornaments crashing to the floor and breaking, and supervise volumes of tinsel being thrown all over the place. It was blissful chaos for us, while my dad probably felt it was the Christmas nightmare! A sense of humor helped keep the festivities memorable.

As adults, we reminisce about all the funny moments we remember as children and it never fails to make us laugh. We are sure that our children are storing up their memories for future story-telling sessions with their children. My siblings and I are blessed to have grown up in a family of storytellers, uncles and aunts who loved a good joke. At every family gathering there are moments where roars of laughter can be heard wafting from table to table. I dare say there are moments during a family eulogy or funeral luncheon when, if you didn't know it, you'd think it was a party of some sorts, rather than a solemn occasion. Even in times of grief, we celebrate with laughter and joyful stories with those we love.

We are all drawn to people who lift us up. Reinhold Niebukr said, "humor is a prelude to faith and laughter is the beginning of prayer." Amen to that! A spiritual life cannot be whole without a sense of humor. It is necessary to living a holy life. Humor is found in the imperfections and humanness of life.

So why is it that people of faith are often stereotyped as humorless? Perhaps, although often well-intentioned, I think we bring the wrath of humorlessness upon ourselves.

When we believe religion is bigger than God, we lose our sense of humanity. Religion becomes an institution of rules and regulations, rather than an anchor for compassion, love, kindness, and service to God and others. Religions serve to bring those of faith together so as to build relationship with God. We come to worship in our humanness, which means we bring all our experiences, prejudices, shortcomings, and joys with us. By taking ourselves too seriously, we risk being joyless in our life experiences. We all know the person who over-thinks things, who is too critical, the one who is so rigid and controlled they seem to have no sense of humor. How about the person who always needs to be right? The person who feels the need to do everything perfectly? They can imprison themselves with details so much so that they lose their sense of humor. It's difficult to be around those people day in and day out. We prefer to be with people who can admit their faults, can laugh at themselves, and can find the joy and humor in the very ordinary experiences of everyday life.

When we read stories about our spiritual ancestors, our personal mentors, heroes, and those we consider great leaders, they all have one thing in common: a sense of humor. They can laugh at a good joke as well as at themselves every once and awhile. Their lives are far from perfect. They endure life's mundane moments, sorrows, and challenges, but their spiritual journey would not be complete without a sense of humor and real joy. When I talk about joy, I don't necessarily mean the "throw your hands up in the air, oh I'm so happy" joy, I mean the kind that's deep inside when we feel at peace. It's that joy that is part of us at birth, given to us by our Creator. Life is too short not to find some "sacred silliness" in each day.

Here are ten things you can do to keep the joy and humor alive inside you:

- Smile. It's at the top of every list. There is a physical reaction in your body when you smile. It makes you feel better.
- Time out. If you are feeling overwhelmed, take a time out. Watch a comedy on TV or a silly movie. Let humor distract you! If you are in a workplace, take a walk outside your office or at least your cubicle, to share a joke with a coworker.
- Spend time with a person who always makes you smile. There is nothing like calling or visiting with a friend who knows you best.
- Read a funny book. Another person's story can lift our mood.
- Visit a funny website.
- Recall humorous moments in your life. Find a family photo album and enjoy!
- Find the humor in the absurd and frustrating. Share your feelings with a trusted confidant. We often can diffuse negative feelings by seeing how seriously we're taking them.
- Write your own jokes or memorize a few good ones. Practice a few good jokes so you're ready to share them when the time is right. Remember, it's all in the delivery!
- Get a group of friends together. Have each one talk about their most embarrassing moment. You will be roaring all night long! One story leads to another.
- Sing a silly childhood song. If you're having a bad day and cannot seem to focus on anything positive, change the tune in your head. Soon you'll be singing a new song!

PERSONAL REFLECTION

What do you think of the idea of "sacred silliness?"

Despite difficult moments in your life, have you discovered blessings in the midst of turmoil that ultimately brought joy and humor into your life?

When was the last time you shared a joke with a friend, belly-laughed, or acted silly? Describe how it made you feel? How do you feel thinking about it again?

What questions, thoughts, reflections arise in you at this time?

Chapter 12

Faithfulness

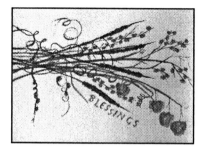

"Consecration is defined as dedication to a divinity...
It implies intentionally participating with the divine.
We can be dedicated to anything: to a task, a cause, a nation.
But we can be consecrated only to God."
Gerald May

While growing up, I was seen as a leader, a go-getter, and a moving force in accomplishing goals once I put my mind to it. I learned it's easier to be faithful when things are going our way; it's when we are tested that we find out how dedicated we are to doing God's will.

Saying I have faith in God is one thing, taking the risk to respond to God's call requires heartfelt action of mind, body, and spirit. After years of battling my obsessive-compulsive behavior patterns, there were many times I felt hopeless and discouraged that I would ever find a solution. I had so many questions and felt as though answers were not forthcoming. Did God abandon me? Did I deserve God's attention? Did I trust that God could rescue me from my self-imposed prison?

At some level, I felt unworthy of God's help. If I couldn't help myself, why should I ask God to intervene? Maybe it was all the years of religious training both at home and in school that convinced me, despite my doubts, that God was the only one I could turn to. A series of events took place that restored my commitment to my faith. Some might say it was serendipitous. I know it was the grace of God and movement of the Spirit that led me to seek recovery. I always believed in God, but honestly, at the time, that was a lot of lip service. It was at my lowest point that I abandoned myself to God's plan. Trusting God's plan began with admitting mine wasn't working so well.

Our local paper had a list of self-help groups that met on a weekly basis. My husband was in the Coast Guard and out to sea, and I thought it would be the perfect opportunity to check out a support meeting without him having to know about it. I was still so embarrassed by my behaviors that I was sure he'd be disgusted if I ever told him what was going on. It was still too painful to reveal those hidden parts of myself that had me feeling such shame.

At the time, I was working as a labor and delivery nurse in one of the local hospitals. One of the officers aboard my husband's ship and his wife were expecting their first child. I had promised her that should she go into labor, especially if the ship was out to sea, I would coach her through the delivery.

Circled on my calendar was the day the support group was meeting. I had promised God and myself I would follow through. I was willing, although not feeling altogether ready. Lo and behold, on the same day of the meeting I received a call early in the morning from our friend telling me she thought she was in labor. I remember midway through the day, as I sat monitoring my friend's contractions, I had a discussion with God quietly in my head. It went something like this: "I know I promised you I would go to the meeting, but I also promised my friend I would stay with her through her delivery. I know you understand." Of course, God understood; he's God! He also clearly understood my fear and denial.

There was a part of me that felt relieved. I now convinced myself I had a good enough excuse not to attend the meeting. God also has a sense of humor, and around five o'clock we received a call that the ship would be in port within the hour. Although my friend's contractions were getting stronger and more regular, it looked as if she'd be able to *hold off going to the hospital until her husband arrived home.*

A tiny voice began to well up inside of me. It insisted that since my husband had duty on the ship, I would still be able to make the evening meeting. Darn that quiet voice!

As my godchild was born that evening in the delivery room, I was being reborn in a second floor room of that same hospital, attending a meeting that forever changed my life.

I sincerely wanted to make changes that would help me become a better person. Despite my fears and ambivalence, grace entered in. My faith was put to the test that day. Would I take the risk and trust God, or make more excuses as I had so many times before? That tiny voice that urged me to follow through and go to the meeting had to be God's urging, because alone I would have chickened out.

We are often like Thomas, the disciple in scripture who earned his reputation by struggling with believing what he could not see. Until he saw Jesus appear to him in the upper room and could place his hands upon his wounds, he would not believe in the Resurrection of his friend, teacher and Lord. The Bible is filled with stories of doubters, of real people who believed in God but were at times unwilling to risk believing what they did not see. That should give us all hope that God does not concern himself with our doubts, but rather with our sincere intention to believe.

Faithfulness does not require perfection, nor is it the absence of doubt, for even the saints were continually challenged. Faithfulness is about remaining loyal to God even in our doubt. It's about steadfastly adhering to our moral compass despite what the world would have us believe. It is about devotion to God through thick and thin, when we're on top and when we're on the bottom, when we can see clearly and when we are blind.

Being faithful means that God calls us together to be nourished spiritually as one body and then disperses the body into different places to do his work on earth. We go about faithful works even when things don't appear to be going so well. There will be times we don't see the fruits of our labor. It's about planting seeds despite those who do not support our efforts or understand our verve. Faithfulness isn't so much a feeling as it is the action of doing what God calls us to do, even when we are discouraged and just not "feeling it." Faithfulness brings us toward holiness.

Ask God in prayer to lead you to a community of people who strive to live faithful lives, perhaps a church community that nourishes your spirit. There are those who would argue that God is everywhere and there is no need for formal religion or attendance at church services. They usually cite busyness, disinterest, boredom, and antiauthoritarian reasons for not wanting to attend faithfully. Some want to be wowed and entertained. If the service isn't delivered with pizzazz, they become turned off. Making excuses about the hypocrites in church, the boring sermons, the rote prayers and the lack of entertainment are very often just that, excuses. Faithfulness calls us beyond excuses. It calls us to service, thanksgiving, and honoring and praising the Divine.

Church isn't about an individual. Faithfulness sets aside our desires in exchange for God's desires for us. God calls us into community. We are God's body for the purpose of living out the gospel message of love, compassion, justice, and peace. God calls us all together and leaves no one behind. God doesn't just call the virtuous and good- deed-doers to worship, he calls the broken, hopeless, and evildoers as well. At Mass, for example, we are gathered around the Word and the Eucharist in celebration of life, love, and sacrifice. Faithfulness means we are being called as witnesses for God. Church is a community response through prayer, song, and thanksgiving to God, the universe and one another.

Someone struggling may need your presence at a church service to encourage them. An elderly person may need their hope renewed by the presence of a young family, a child may need a role model to look up to, or the prayers intended for a struggling world need a collective voice. There is a sign as you leave the parking lot of my church that reads: Entering Mission Territory. That is where God takes us, beyond ourselves and into the lives of those who need us.

We need to build up a resistance toward negativity and doubt. Surround yourself with hopeful people who are positive about what God is doing in your life and theirs.

Improving our prayer life by simply talking with God on a regular basis settles our minds and bodies and opens us up to an affirming Holy Presence in our life. Companioning with God assures us that whatever comes our way, we are never alone. He is faithful to us even when our faithfulness to him wavers.

Our faith will be tested. Hold tightly to the promise that God is walking with us through every one of life's difficulties and challenges. God never loses sight of us despite our own uncertainty at times. Let God find you in your times of doubt.

Faithfulness and love go hand in hand. Every world religion or spiritual practice places love above all else. Becoming more faithful in our marriages, family life, relationships, work life, extracurricular activities, vocations and prayer life begins with putting God's will at the center of it all. Faithfulness to God's will brings about love.

PERSONAL REFLECTION

What does faithfulness to God mean to you?

When has your faith been tested? Describe.

Do you trust God's plan for you? What challenges do you experience in your daily faith life?

What is one thing or one area in your life you feel called to trust to God right now?

What questions, thoughts, or reflections arise in you at this time?

Chapter 13

Teachability

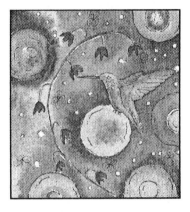

*"There is only one thing worth being concerned about.
Mary has discovered it- and I won't take it away from her."*
Luke 10:42

During the Lenten season, Catholics are challenged to listen closely for God's voice in the experiences of daily life. We focus our attention on fasting, almsgiving, and prayer. This helps remind us of our dependence on God. We take a look at our own weaknesses and become willing to ask God to help us change negative patterns in our lives. It is a time to recommit ourselves to God and ready ourselves to become an "Alleluia" people; people who desire to live in the hope and light of the Resurrection.

One of my commitments during this particular Lenten season was quite simple. In the morning, I wanted to sit quietly and reflect on scripture before I went to work. I thought this was the perfect way to enrich my prayer life. During the first week of Lent, I was faithful to the morning ritual. The second week, I was distracted by a few issues, and by the third week, I had pretty much abandoned my morning practice. I was frustrated with myself and felt as though I was letting God and myself down. Surely, I thought my Lenten experience would suffer as a result of my inability to stick with my promised ritual.

It was a particularly busy time in the campus ministry office at school. Students seemed to be coming into my office daily with issues and concerns that took a long time to process. Feeling a bit drained, I looked forward to a week of spring break.

Only a couple of days into the break, I received a call from a senior student with whom I worked closely during his four years of high school. His family and personal journey had seen its share of rocky times. He and I seemed to hit it off from the start, and built a bond of trust over the years.

As soon as I heard his voice, I knew something was not right. He explained that he was at the hospital with his mother. Apparently, his mother made a suicide attempt and it was he who found her unconscious in a car parked in their garage. He explained details and said that she was going to make a full recovery physically. Since he did not have a healthy relationship with his father, whom he rarely saw, his mother meant the world to him. He understood his mother's mental health issues better than most young men his age. Despite some confusion and resentment about his mother's condition, he loved her with all his heart. His compassion and empathy clearly were a driving force in his relationship with his mom.

After we spoke, I thought about the long-term implications of this incident on my student. Were his coping skills sufficient to handle the intense pain, fear, and perhaps anger his mother's suicide attempt would stir up in him? What would the following weeks bring in terms of his ability to remain focused in school and graduate? What kinds of support would he need? Would his faith in God be shaken? After all, it was he who described cradling his mother's head in his arms as he begged God not to let her die.

Upon returning to school after the spring break, he appeared in my office first thing Monday morning. I understood that he did not want to lose control of his emotions in school. I encouraged him to feel his *way through whatever was on his mind and asked a few open-ended questions to allow him to share at his comfort level. He shared a little, and, choking down his emotions, became quiet. We sat together and allowed the silence for a good period of time.*

A presentation I'd recently watched by author and speaker Ronald Rolheiser came to my mind in the silence. In it, he described Jesus' invitation to us, to come to him in our brokenness. He talked about Christ identifying with us in our suffering. He went on to describe a painting by Holman Hunt entitled, "The Light of the World." It is an allegorical painting in which Jesus is standing in the darkness with a lantern in one hand and raising his other hand to knock on a door. The long-unopened door is overgrown with weeds. There is no handle on the door; therefore, it must be opened from the inside.

This is where my memory of Rolheiser's interpretation gets fuzzy; however, it's how I recalled his explanation that was helpful in that moment. He refers to a line from the Apostle's Creed that says, "He descended into hell." I've read that line a thousand times over and never did it make as much sense as it did when Rolheiser spoke about God being able to descend into our personal hell. How many times are we, like Hunt's allegorical painting implies, behind the door, refusing to let God in? How often do we allow pain, suffering, resentment, and loneliness grow like weeds upon our closed hearts? And, how many times, despite the door being locked and our unwillingness to let God in, has God by his grace descended into our private hell to comfort us? How often has someone appeared during difficult moments to comfort us in our time of need?

Before he left my office, I shared the image of the locked door with this young man. I suggested that God was reaching into his mother's private hell when she felt desperate and hopeless. And perhaps God was reaching into his hell of confusion, anger, and pain as well.

After exchanging an embrace of support and sending him on his way, I felt a rush of emotion. I pushed down a desire to do the impossible, to somehow find a way to take away this young man's pain and confusion. Instead, with my whole heart and mind, I prayed. I turned him and his family over to the care of the God I knew, who reaches into the depths we cannot go alone.

I learned something that day as I prayed to God. Maybe my Lenten journey wasn't exactly as I had planned it to be. Although I had good intentions to faithfully sit in prayer every morning, perhaps God had other plans. I was living into my prayer this particular Lenten season through the experiences within my office. Every student with whom I shared was a part of my prayer experience.

You may be familiar with Luke's biblical account of two sisters, Martha and Mary, who, upon receiving a visit from Jesus and his disciples, respond quite differently to the situation in which they find themselves. Both women were deeply devoted to their faith and welcomed guests and strangers "as if they were entertaining angels without realizing it." (Hebrews 13:2)

Martha paid attention to all the fine details, making sure their guests were able to relax and have something to eat and drink. She's the gal who dotted all her I's and crossed all her T's. Martha would have been the perfect host. She reminds me of the modern day Martha Stewart many of us would like to emulate, and yet, while trying, fall just a little short. If only we could decorate our tables with fresh-cut flowers that match funky china, place cloth napkins monogrammed with our guests' initials on tables, along with glitter candles tucked inside topiaries that hold brightly designed place cards for each guest. We would serve smoked trout and garlic cream hors d'oeuvres, and our herb-encrusted rib roast and artichoke turnovers would bake in the oven as we displayed our salted caramel six-layer chocolate cake for dessert on the dainty matching cake plate we recently designed and fired in ceramics class! Martha is the do-er, perhaps a little bit of a perfectionist. Don't get me wrong; we all love and need the do-ers of this world. There is a place for Martha in all of us. She's feisty, driven, creative, competent, and organized.

As she bustles around the house, Luke's Martha looks over to see her sister Mary sitting at the feet of Jesus. I imagine that Mary is intently listening to the stories and wisdom shared by Jesus. She rubs his tired feet with oil and perfume, totally enthralled with the man she has come to understand with her heart. The student is clearly attentive to the teacher. But this isn't sitting well with Martha, who is doing all the work. She's got to be thinking: "Are you kidding me? I've got all this work and you're not even going to lift a finger to help me?" Martha's insides are burning and she probably feels like she got the short end of the stick! More than likely feeling some resentment, she approaches Jesus and points out that Mary is doing nothing to help her prepare the dinner. She suggests that Jesus should let her sister know how unfair that is. What is Jesus' response? "There is only one thing worth being concerned about, Martha." Jesus points out that Mary has chosen to be present to something that is more valuable in that moment. This is what we call a teachable moment.

Have you had your share of Martha moments? Times you've been so busy working that you've not taken time to enjoy the process? Have you been so focused on what you thought you needed to accomplish that you neglected to notice the little gifts presented along the way? Have worries and concerns consumed your thoughts and left little time for prayer? Have you paid too much attention to what others expect, rather than trusting God's plan for you?

Jesus [God] is speaking to all of us. He is calling us to take a break from the "busy-ness" of our lives to spend time with him. We are all called to spend time sitting at the feet of Jesus. Taking a break to quiet ourselves and to listen to the inner voice of God renews and encourages us in our work, home, and spiritual lives. Being "teachable" requires that we are willing to acknowledge we don't have all the answers and that we remain open to new thoughts and ideas. We remain open to God's plan for us when we:

- Keep an open mind.
- Listen.
- Pay attention.
- Look for new opportunities.
- Rather than judge, seek the lesson.
- Surround yourself with "seekers."

Whether we move toward learning experiences or let them come to us, we must pay close attention, listen, and keep an open mind. Whether painful or joyous, drawn out or short-lived, ordinary or extraordinary, life holds a treasure trove of lessons for us to receive. Let your attitude be one of desire, a desire to continue seeking the Holy One in all things.

PERSONAL REFLECTION

Describe a teachable moment. What did you learn about yourself? Others? God? Explain.

How does your life mirror Martha's? How does your life mirror Mary's?

What spiritual disciplines—for example, prayer, meditation or exercise—help you to remain teachable?

What questions, thoughts, reflections arise in you at this time?

Chapter 14

Meditation

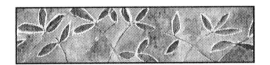

*"A life without a lonely place, that is,
a life without a quiet center,
easily becomes destructive."*
Henri J.M. Nouwen

A few years ago my previous spiritual director sensed that I was feeling unsettled and a bit frazzled during a session. We stopped and processed what might be buried beneath the feelings. He then suggested that I close my eyes as he brought me through a simple meditation. He repeated these words slowly until my body, mind, and spirit felt calm and centered:

Be Still and Know that I Am God

Be Still and Know that I Am

Be Still and Know

Be Still

Be

Since that time I've used these words taken from Psalm 46:10 on many occasions. It is a reminder to me that God can do things I feel unable to do alone. The spiritual calm that comes over me does not mean the absence of problems or concerns; instead, it means a steady and deep commitment to placing my trust in a God who loves me unconditionally.

Meditation

Most people would find jogging on a track quite boring. While I too enjoy days when I can jog in the woods or along a winding path, I find the repetitive action of jogging on a track quite soothing. It's like praying a rosary. I switch one lane every quarter mile around the track. There is nothing to think about, no cars, hills, or holes to be mindful of. It's like being on autopilot for a few miles. My mind rests and I allow God to fill me up with whatever I need to hear. Sometimes it's the birds or sounds of nature, or a song or prayer. There are times my mind wanders in creative directions and I think of things to write for my webpage or ideas for a new program or painting. Other times, God works with me to evaluate actions I may want to take when working on relationship issues at work, home, or within the family.

I enjoy dabbling in watercolors. Creating a canvas filled with color and whimsy takes some concentration and creativity. Some days when I enter the creative space in which I paint, it's as if a switch goes on in my head. I see light, shape, color, and rhythm. Picking up a brush is for me a way to meditate. I get lost in the creative process. Again, it's all repetition. Brush in hand, dip into water, mix in the paint, and apply to the paper. It's so easy to get caught up in the movement and shading and texture that I forget about time. My mind and body is an open channel to the creative process. Worries and concerns seem a million miles away.

On a warm spring or summer day, the gardens around my home are meditation spaces for which I find escape and peace. With tools in hand, I plant and weed flowers. Hours can go by as I dig and dabble in nature's playground. Can this be meditative? Bathed with the sunshine of the Spirit, attuned to nature's music, emptied of all concerns, my gardens are sacred spaces of joy and solitude.

I find it difficult to sit in the lotus position and meditate; quite frankly, my hips are usually screaming in pain. Since that is what we often envision meditation to be, you can breathe easy, because it has less to do with body position and more to do with your inner disposition.

Meditation is a repetitive practice that empties the self of self. It is emptying the mind of all its busy activity so that God can fill it with what we need. And what we need from God is not always information for doing something, but rather simple delight in just being present to something beautiful, creative, or natural. For instance, a quiet morning walk can indeed be an opportunity for meditation. The rhythm of your steps in concert with relaxed breathing may place you in closer conscious contact with God. Before you know it, you are allowing God to fill you with wonder, with attention toward those things God wishes you to notice, with thoughts that quiet your mind.

No two people meditate exactly the same way, precisely because our physical, emotional, and mental responses to relaxation are unique to us. Some people meditate to a rhythm or beat, some to soothing music, others in complete silence. Some people like movement while others appreciate stillness. Meditation may take place in a group setting or while a person is alone.

My husband feels he meditates best while fishing. To him, a day on the river is completely refreshing and calming. Concerns about work and deadlines are replaced by the attention toward small tasks and the natural world around him. He often tells me, "I'm going to the church on the river bank today!" Not so far-fetched—the apostles seemed to find comfort on the banks of rivers.

A common way to begin the practice of meditation is to find a space that is comfortable and relaxing for you. Perhaps a quiet space outdoors in nature, such as a garden, a lake or river, a pool, a waterfall, the woods, or the ocean would work for you. Others may find a chair, room, chapel, or some other indoor space more relaxing. Give yourself five minutes of quiet time at first. Close your eyes and become aware of your breathing. Some people focus on releasing tension in all parts of their body working from head to toe, others remain focused on the rhythm of their breathing. Still others focus on a mantra, a repeated series of affirming words, or visualize a beautiful, safe place in which to concentrate. The experiences vary from person to person. As you practice meditation, you may find yourself craving more quiet time with the Divine.

There is no right way to meditate, so how will you know when it's working? Chances are that if you are practicing meditation, you will notice an increased energy and creativity. Your moods will be lighter and calmer. You'll be paying more attention to what is happening in the outside world—seasonal changes, the beauty, smells, sights, and sounds of the natural world. You will pay more attention to your actions and how you say things to people. You will find yourself more relaxed, kinder, less reactive, and more attentive toward others. Concentration at work, in the home, and toward daily tasks should increase.

The most important benefit of meditation is a closer relationship with God. By letting go of the distractions, we are better able to discern God's will in our life. When our mind is quiet, we are more likely to hear the truth. In the stillness, we are more capable of authenticity and therefore have more capacity to love God, others, and ourselves.

I once heard meditation described as the Divine art of paying attention to the moments of our lives. How beautiful is that? And, don't you just want a piece of it?
It begins with practice. Today is as good a day as any!

PERSONAL REFLECTION

Do you have preconceived ideas about meditation that may be keeping you from attempting the practice? Describe.

Describe ways you have meditated that are calming and energizing for you.

Find a quiet space and take five minutes of silence. (You may want to set a timer.)
Pay attention to your breathing. What happened during that five minutes? Describe.

What questions, thoughts, reflections arise in you at this time?

Chapter 15

Discipline

"For God gave us a spirit not of fear
but of power and love and self-control."
2 Timothy 1:7

Discipline is that dirty little word that for me conjured up thoughts of pain and relentless work. Upon hearing the word, I thought of punishment or deprivation of some kind.

Making a decision to take a new path in my life was not entirely without doubts, fear, and discomfort. Changes had to be made and a plan of action totally opposite of what I had known was necessary.

The first decision I made was to ask for help. After years of believing I needed to take care of this obsessive-compulsive behavior on my own, it wasn't easy to enlist the help of others. I made a commitment to God that I would find a support group in the area and attend a meeting. I had exhausted all of my own schemes and plans. Since all I tried had failed, I was finally willing to reach out for help.

Contrary to my belief that I lacked enough willpower, I learned that, indeed, I had plenty of willpower. The problem, it was suggested to me, was that I was confusing my will with God's will for me. Finding healthy solutions to help me deal with unhealthy emotions and desires required a life-changing perspective. These steps were part of a disciplined approach toward wholeness and well-being.

I was well acquainted with what it took to get into good physical condition. I knew the importance of exercise, eating a balanced diet, drinking plenty of water, strengthening the core, and getting rest. A certain amount of discipline is necessary to keep our bodies fit. Intellectually, I knew all these things, yet I failed to implement them into my life on a consistent basis.

Physical discipline alone was not enough. Emotional and spiritual discipline was necessary as well. If I believed God was in charge of my thoughts, my instincts, my intuition, and my ability to reason and make choices, then I had to relinquish control to God. I had to begin by trusting that God could and would move my mind, body, and spirit toward health. Actually, that was God's desire for me. All I needed was right inside of me through his Spirit. Through these gifts of reason, intuition, instinct, and choice I could allow God to help me find the right amount and kind of discipline necessary to heal physically, emotionally, and spiritually.

I no longer viewed discipline as a necessary evil but, rather, life sustaining. Discipline was no longer something I should do, but something I desired. Putting God's plan into action was far more challenging and rewarding than I ever imagined. God's plan was not about shoulds and musts. It was about noticing my responses and behaviors. I could discern with his help what worked best and make my choices.

I made my share of poor choices throughout this process. A poor choice was just that, a poor choice. It was an opportunity to learn something new about myself, others, or God, and to begin again. It was not an opportunity to beat myself up as I had in the past.

When our children do or say something that causes others harm, we lovingly, yet firmly, discipline them, so that the next time they are in a similar situation, they are more cautious. A budget may be a necessary form of discipline when we find that our overspending is causing credit card debt. Eating fried and salty foods may cause a rise in blood pressure; therefore, dietary discipline may be necessary. Involvement in the drama of a work situation may cause upheaval and distrust among co-workers. Refusing to participate in gossip may be a disciplined way of dealing with the situation.

Much like our physical bodies, our souls crave spiritual conditioning. How much time do you spend a day in caring for your spiritual fitness? A better understanding of the word certainly may help to lead us toward embracing rather than shunning it.

The word discipline comes from the thirteenth-century Latin word "disciplina" which means teaching or learning, or "discipulus" which means pupil. In the Christian tradition, we see Jesus teaching his chosen followers or disciples. His disciples, like each of us, endured many obstacles along life's journey. Perhaps if we open our minds to the idea of learning, we could better accept discipline as part of our spiritual practice. After all, like the disciples, we are learning to depend on God's will.

Spiritual discipline is a lifelong process. It is a process that places us in the role of the pupil. We are going to make mistakes and will experience desert periods where we feel dry and uninspired. We will find ourselves sidetracked by life's distractions and sorrows and feel like giving up. There are times we feel like life has dealt us some insurmountable odds.

The wonderful paradox about spiritual fitness is that while it does require our attention, we don't have to go through mental and physical gymnastics to become more fit. It's not about taking more control; it's about letting go. Repetition is not only encouraged but also necessary. Mistakes are an opportunity for growth. God becomes our strength coach! And God never gives up on us.

An addict in recovery knows well the meaning of right use of power. Addicts fight between their desire for whatever fills the empty hole of the soul and their desire to do the next right thing. At the point where the addict finally understands that filling the empty hole over and over again with the same negative habit is destructive, he may surrender to a process of spiritual discipline. That is, he may surrender himself to a Power greater than himself for direction in his life.

So, too, for all who find themselves attached to negative patterns and habits, rather than self dependence, we are called to depend on God's will for us. My sponsor used to say about the Twelve-Step Program: it is not a self-improvement program, it is a "let God improve you" program. Most would agree that without a Higher Power in our lives there isn't a chance of self-improvement.

So, then, we are called to let God improve us. We are called as disciples to stay alert, to watch, to listen, and to learn. Jesus, for example, upon gathering his disciples, didn't set about calling on perfectly holy men. Rather he called on men who had some issues. The same goes for us. God calls on us in our brokenness and is passionate about our being restored to wholeness. After all, he created us for the purpose of serving others in His name. We can best serve others when we are authentically who God created us to be. It takes spiritual discipline to avoid the temptations of the world around us and to remain who it is we are called to be.

We don't blindly follow a set of rules and regulations. We begin to trust gut instincts, intuitions, and soft whispers that are God speaking to us, through us, within us. We begin to follow spiritual practices that may help us to work toward our goal of freedom. That goal is to be the person God is calling us to be, free from attachments and free from our self imposed prisons of "shoulds."

Is this easy? No, it's not easy, but it is simple. We surrender our lives to God. God in turn empowers us to make decisions. God, who desires only goodness for us, is really rooting for us to make healthy decisions. God places people in our lives to help us reach our goals. We need to pay attention to who those people are. We are free to make choices. Sometimes we have to tighten up our boundaries. It helps us to become better people. Overindulgence in anything is usually not a good thing.

These are just some of the actions I have taken over the past several years to help me remain spiritually fit and always learning. There is no expectation of perfection. Instead, move forward with the idea of progressing toward becoming your most authentic self, the person God has created you to become.

Set one inspirational goal for your day. Rather than a harsh list of "don'ts" or unrealistic promises, make a commitment to a small change. Become a student once again. Being mindful of your goal, open yourself to learning all you can. Listen to suggestions; allow others to help guide you. Initially, you may try to do what seems to work for others; eventually, you will find what works for you. A daily discipline may emerge that provides structure, yet flexibility. Notice the areas of your life that could use some improvement.

Eat foods that nourish your body.

Attend a support meeting if necessary and useful. They are often listed in community newspapers or online.

Journal. Get a cheap spiral notebook. If you get a pretty journal, you may tend to write only pretty things. Write what needs to be written. This is an opportunity to be honest, to dream, to create, to give expression to your deepest desires and feelings.

Set aside time for prayer and meditation.

Phone someone who will listen to you, someone you can trust to be honest with you, a person who will support you but won't tell you only what you want to hear.

Exercise daily (walking, jogging, yoga, strength training, swimming, kayaking. Just move your body).

Find a faith community. There isn't a perfect one out there. Why? Humans are involved. Move past old resentments. God is calling.

Find a community service project that interests you. Stop procrastinating. When you hear or see the call, answer it as if responding to an invitation from God.

Discipline

Attend workshops that nourish your spirit. Call a local retreat center. You cannot believe what is happening so close to home. There are day programs, directed retreats, silent retreats, evening reflections, spiritual direction and more. For example, these were some of the topics offered over six months at a retreat house in my area: Contemplative Stargazing; Labyrinth Walk; Wake-Up Conversations in Spirituality: Common Ground in World Religions; Fire and the Holy Spirit; A Prayerful Pause; Centering Prayer: Beyond Conversation with God; Giving Thanks. There is something for everyone.

Read scripture and other inspirational material.

Occasional fasting. This does not mean from food only. Fasting is a way of cleansing the overindulgences from our lives. Clean out the closets, the basement, and the attic. Rid yourself of excess. Assess your behaviors. If you find a negative behavior is being repeated perhaps replace it with a positive action.

Meet with a spiritual director once a month. Share your spiritual journey with someone who is trained and certified to companion with you. A retreat center can refer you to someone.

Spend time alone (at the beach, in the woods, under a tree). Five minutes each day will establish a healthy pattern.

Discipline can reap many rewards. You may be thinking, "I'm too busy to follow through on some of these actions." If you're too busy to take the time to nurture your relationship with God, you're too busy! Life isn't a dress rehearsal; it's the real thing. Be willing to set aside time to become a disciple, a pupil of the Beloved. There is so much we have to learn. Open yourself to the possibilities.

God never said it would be easy, but he did say he would always be with us. Trust that. The result of healthy spiritual discipline is freedom to be who God is calling you to be.

PERSONAL REFLECTION

What meaning does the word "discipline" have in your life?

What present disciplines are effective in your daily life? How do they improve your physical life? Emotional life? Spiritual life?

What areas of your life are in need of physical, emotional, or spiritual discipline?

Who are the people you rely on for support? How do they help you through the daily disciplines that lead you to freedom?

What questions, thoughts, reflections arise in you at this time?

Chapter 16

Flexibility

*"It's easier to think outside the box
if you don't draw one around yourself."*
Jason Kravitz

*They say one good way to make God laugh is to tell him your plans
for the day! Being a Type A personality has its benefits and drawbacks.
I've set plenty of goals in my lifetime, some that from the very
beginning were only attainable in a "perfect world" scenario. That
being said, I'm learning, sometimes the hard way, that adjustments
must be made. Having a daily plan of action can be a powerful tool,
so long as I understand that life has a way of throwing kinks into the
best-intentioned plans. My ability to be flexible often determines the
extent of my inner peace. As I mature, I find myself less willing to live
by rules that offer no flexibility. I am more willing to bend and move
rather than resist or hold my ground on matters that really aren't so
important.*

*It's not always the big things that seem to snare us in the web of
temporary insanity; it's the everyday things. Take, for example, the
day I was scheduled to give two programs at a retreat center an hour*

from my home. I woke up jazzed about the presentation and looking forward to the day ahead. After eating my breakfast and making a few last minute adjustments, I was out the door. One turn of the key in my car ignition told me that my day was not going to go as planned. My battery was dead.

Can we see ourselves in this type of scenario? Panic sets in and we immediately shut down or fly off the handle. We wish we would act like a normally adjusted person, and instead, find ourselves overreacting to the slightest kink in the plans! On this particular day, I calmly called the car dealership and they sent a tow truck and changed my battery. I explained the urgency of getting to work and they were able to help me.

Just a week after this incident, I was driving home from an appointment on a very windy and rainy day. It was four days before Christmas and people were coming for lunch. I was looking forward to a relaxing afternoon catching up with friends.

As I drove into my driveway, I was shocked to see a huge pine tree had fallen on our house. It was hanging over my roof and covering one side of the house. My heart sank, but rather than flying into a tizzy, I calmly called my husband at work and explained the situation. He came home, and together we took pictures, examined the interior and exterior of the house for damage. We contacted the insurance agency and a tree service. Although my day didn't go exactly as planned, I managed to move through it by asking God to help me to remain calm. There were things I could do and things I could not change. I prayed for the willingness to go with the flow rather than put up walls of anger.

In both situations, what surprised me was my response to what would have inevitably sent me into hysteria in the past. I centered myself in God. I asked for a peaceful heart in the midst of chaos. I was able to make the necessary adjustments to move forward in a healthy manner.

The more we learn to trust the process and flow of life, the more our capacity and desire for inner peace grows. Making adjustments rather than overreacting helps us feel physically, emotionally and spiritually more balanced. To take a breath and think things through before over-

reacting seems a rather simple suggestion, and it is. If we could stop and slow our breathing and ask God to help us, more often than not, the stuff we begin to spew out of our mouths might just be swallowed instead of spoken. We may find our bodies and minds relaxing and trying to find solutions, rather than creating more problems. We would accept the reality as it is dealt to us and make attempts to work through, rather than around our problems.

Improving our emotional and spiritual flexibility is much like the athlete trying to maintain his or her physical flexibility.

First we must warm up. Get loose. Open your mind to the possibilities of new alternatives.

Extend the time you stretch and loosen up. Practice letting go of old habits and ideas that restrict your intellectual and spiritual movement.

Practice good form. An athlete will tell you that flexibility begins with strength in the core. Start from your center. Remain focused in God. Pay attention to what your inner self is feeling and trust your instincts. Rather than doing what you've always done, check your gut instincts and see if the Spirit is moving you in a new direction, offering a creative solution or enriching what is already there.

Take a deep breath. Inhale and let the Spirit move with and through you. Rather than reacting to a situation on impulse, settle yourself with some quiet breaths. Relaxing helps us to open our minds.

Inviting someone into the process can help us relax. We do not have to make decisions alone. Affirmation from a trusted friend or spiritual director, scripture or spiritual material may touch us in ways that open our minds to a new way of approaching a situation or problem.

Massage often helps athletes to loosen up tense muscles. They also rely on warm showers, baths, and saunas to relax. A smile, humor, or a gentle hug may go a long way toward softening the edges when someone is determined their way is the only way. Rather than going on the defense we can offer an alternative to rigidness.

What are some of the signs of inflexibility? We commonly show signs of irritation, anger and perhaps outbursts, when things don't go our way. We begin to believe our opinions matter more than those of others. Our minds convince us we are the sole possessors of the truth. We find ourselves incapable of adapting to new rules or a different set of plans. We insist on always being right. We delude ourselves into thinking we are somehow superior to others. We may notice old ideas aren't working, but because of fear, we refuse to look at new ones.

Rigidity is the opposite of flexibility. It creates chaos within us. It holds fast to the idea that our way is the only way. When our habits, ideas, and attitudes become set in stone we find it difficult to flow with life's rhythm. The physical world is an ever-changing mass of movement. Things are created, live out their life, die, leave an imprint, and then something is born and the cycle continues. Nature and people follow this cycle. Ideas and attitudes follow this cycle. Since change is inevitable we must be willing to bend and move along with the natural cycles in our lives. Think of how many times during the course of our day we are asked to compromise, to change direction, to re-evaluate or to make alternate plans. Our response to these shifts speaks about our capacity to be flexible. A peaceful heart, molded and shaped by God, is far more important than any rigid opinion or attitude we may have.

Flexibility is imperative to a maturing spiritual life. It does not mean we shy away from our beliefs and traditions, but that we extend tolerance to those who come to God in ways that are different from ours. We want to lead those without faith toward God, rather than turn them away. We learn to share ideas and find common ground, holy ground. It is allowing each individual to be shaped and molded by God rather than trying to force our ways upon another person. And sometimes we need to be flexible with the way God teaches and directs us! It's not always how we think he should do it!

No one says this is an easy task. Changes, especially those that are unexpected or sudden, can be uncomfortable and sometimes downright painful.

However, change is the very thing that creates new learning experiences and helps us to grow. When our desires are in sync with God's desires for us, we experience an inner peace and contentment that is not dependent on the outside world. Flexibility doesn't mean we have to compromise our values, but rather to understand that not everyone will relate to our values in a similar manner. Being flexible helps us to soften the edges. It takes away rigidity. It allows us to move with the natural rhythm of our life and allows others to move in theirs. Flexibility does not demand conformity; rather it encourages goodness, tolerance, and openness.

Our safety net is in God because it is a constant we can rely upon. Having faith does not mean my life is without chaos; rather it means that when I trust God, the chaos that exists does not have to affect my inner peace.

PERSONAL REFLECTION

Describe a circumstance when your ability to be flexible created a more positive outcome. What have been the costs of your inflexibility?

What does it mean to you to "soften the edges" in some of your daily decision-making?

What questions, thoughts, or reflections arise in you at this time?

Chapter 17

Responsibility (Respondability)

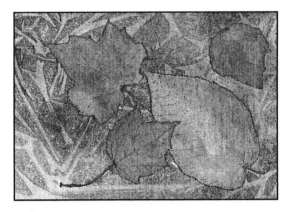

"The greatest defect God, if we let Him, will remove from our lives is the shortcoming of egotism. In our hearts we will be unable to take credit for the improvements in our lives. We will give credit where credit is due, to God whom we trusted to take away our shortcomings no matter what they may turn out to be...
Instead of being responsible,
we will have become respondable."
excerpt from "The Twelve Steps to Happiness" by Joe Klaas

While growing up, I was taught to be responsible for my actions. It was my responsibility to study hard and get good grades, my responsibility to treat people with respect and kindness, and to put forth an effort worthy of consideration for a good job someday. Success was my reward for being a responsible person.

My inability to control my overeating, starving, and binging left me feeling totally irresponsible. If someone didn't like me, I somehow felt responsible for changing his or her mind. Failures, no matter why they occurred, were surely my responsibility. I thought that if I were just more responsible, things would go as I had planned. Somehow the notion that I could magically satisfy personal expectations, and those of others, if I were just a little more responsible, chained me in a prison of self-doubt. If things didn't work out, I had no one to blame but myself. When my self-inflated ego got in the way, I thought I had control, over people, places, and things. I'm pretty sure God was patiently waiting for me to learn a sufficient amount of humility, so as to let go of my need to control.

Being a responsible young woman, I dutifully attended to my school-work. I was intent on becoming the best nurse I could be. Living a faithful life and serving my community seemed like admirable goals.

I thought I was on the right track and doing all the things that would help me reach my goals. And, in fact, my intentions were mostly good. Then, confronted with my own insane behavior around my addiction, I questioned how responsible a person I really was. A responsible person, after all, does not hide and steal food, tell lies to cover up her own actions, blame others, and continue to do the same things over and over again, seemingly failing at every turn. How could someone whose life looked so together on the outside feel so irresponsible and out of control on the inside?

Luckily, I had a mentor who helped me to understand the difference between feeling responsible for everything in my life and being" respondable" to God. He suggested that I build a relationship with my Higher Power and from there I would learn to respond to God's will for my life. If I wanted recovery, part of the process was to learn to turn my life completely over to a Power greater than myself. My first question was, "OK...so what part am I responsible for?"

Initially, the idea of giving up control and putting my complete trust in God, whom I felt had much bigger concerns than mine, wasn't easy.

For sure, I wanted the peace and contentment I'd seen in those with recovery. How could I possibly become responsible enough to manage it? Believing in God was the easy part. Letting go of everything and trusting God to be responsible for my life was difficult. Despite the not-so-great job I seemed to be doing managing my life, just how do I let go and trust God?

I began by trusting others who offered hope and had been down this road. These people were God "with skin on" to me. One day at a time, I made a conscious decision to give my day over to God. I said something like this, "God, today I am yours; please help me to do and say what I'm supposed to do and say, and to not do and say what I'm not supposed to do and say." I decided that whatever happened in my day was God's responsibility. God would get all the glory and all the blame. Since I wasn't sure about the whole question of responsibility, I wasn't going to take blame or credit. I'd just give it all to God. Day after day, I practiced letting go of things I could not change and asked God to help me make changes where it was possible.

I put down the two-by-four I had used for so long to beat up on myself. No longer did I need to judge and place blame on myself. It was all in God's hands. This sounds a bit simplistic, but over time this idea of letting go of the stuff of life changed my perspective. I had spent so much time beating myself up about decisions I made; there was no time to love myself. This gave me a reprieve. I imagined God had a wonderful set of shoulders and a great sense of humor and understood my sincere plea to let go of the need to control everything!

Basically, when I reviewed my day, whatever my choices, I accepted them as part of God's plan. If the choices I made resulted in opportunity to serve God and others, I was grateful. Choices that led to growth experiences were welcomed and satisfying. When, on the other hand, my choices led me into painful experiences, I avoided the blame game. Rather, I began to allow myself to feel the discomfort and work through it or be with it, until God led me to a solution or new understanding. Since God was responsible and God isn't wrong, my response was to trust the plan. God could always inspire me to get back on track. After all, getting off track temporarily isn't such a bad thing in the end. It teaches me a whole lot about myself.

Responsibility (Respondability)

Trying to remove our shortcomings is simply impossible to do by our own will power. We act responsibly when we humbly ask God to take away those things that he wants to remove from us and to leave what he feels is necessary to serve him. Therefore, if God wants us to be leaders, he will give us the power necessary to lead, but with the expectation that we not misuse that power. If he wants us to share our ministry with others, he will give us the right use of words and actions that might benefit others. If God wants us to have material wealth, he will give us what we need to attain wealth along with a generous spirit to share that wealth with others. If God wants us to do certain work, he will provide us with the skills to perform our work so that we are able to reach our greatest potential.

So what are we responsible for?

We are called to be "respondable" to God. We can open ourselves and listen deep within for God's voice. It may come in a roar or a whisper. Perhaps we'll feel the movement of the Spirit inspiring us. God may place someone in our lives to encourage us or to share his or her path with us. Everything we need to problem-solve, to improve our lives, to change habits, to overcome obstacles, and to become the authentic person we are called to be is within us, ready to be accessed through God's grace and power. We no longer need to be responsible when God is in charge of our lives. Instead, we become "respondable" to God's will for us. This idea of "respondability" may not come naturally at first. After all, for many of us, the idea that we pull ourselves up by our bootstraps still makes sense. The part we often forget is that we do not do that alone. It takes God's help.

Are you ready to humble yourself before the Creator and allow God to shape and mold you, on his timetable? The remarkable irony about surrender is that once we begin to think in terms of our responses *to* God rather than our need to be responsible *for* everything in our lives, the more people comment on how responsibly we handle things in our lives. This may be one of life's wonderful paradoxes.

Chapter 18

Willingness

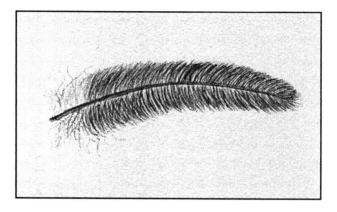

"Be willing to be a beginner every single morning."
Meister Eckhart

I still remember the image of my oldest son learning to take his first steps. Of course, it didn't happen in one day. First, he found his hands and feet through movement. When he learned to rock from side to side, it was as if he was quite pleased to see his world expanding all around him. There were objects to reach that made new sounds and colors that caught his attention. One day, quite by accident, he reached and rocked so confidently that he flipped himself over. The more he saw, the more he wanted to touch. And so he found if he pushed up on his arms and knees, he could move closer to what he desired. Rocking forward, he fell on his face, yet each time he practiced, he inched his body further along.

One day, he pulled himself along until he reached the couch. With his arms extended, he inched his butt closer and closer until he could pull himself up by holding onto the couch. After spending time comfortably hanging on to the couch, he took a risk and let go. He fell to the floor. It scared him, so the next few times as he pulled himself up, he cautiously held onto the couch.

Something inside him wanted to risk again and again, until one day, when he let go, he was standing up straight. The first few times, he wobbled to and fro, but within days, he was standing for longer and longer periods on his own. He even practiced holding a toy and standing at the same time. Finally, with my arms outstretched and some reassurance, he took a few steps toward me. Mom and dad cheered, so he tried again and again until he was putting one foot in front of the other. As time went on he became more sure-footed and stable.

Oh, to be child-like and willing to risk the unknown. Can we say we are entirely ready to be led by God to become who we are created to be? Are we willing to risk being out of our comfort zone? Are we willing to take measures to right our wrongs? Do we think we have all the answers, or are we willing to admit there is a lot we can learn?

The point is not that we will never have doubts, but rather, we become willing to trust God to lead us in the direction we are meant to go despite our doubts. We'll never be one hundred percent ready, so we might as well be willing to give it our best shot! Since our life's journey is not revealed to us ahead of time, our willingness to put one foot in front of the other is sometimes the only thing we can do. Like a child, we often must bring the body and allow the mind to follow.

The word willingness contains the word "will." Since we are born with a will, we must assume it is of God; it is a gift. And like all gifts from God, it is our choice as to how we will use it. If we conform our will to God's, we will find peace and contentment. If we allow self-will to run riot, we may find ourselves feeling discontented and disconnected from God, others, and ourselves.

How do we become willing to say "Yes!" to those things that are life-affirming and "No!" to those that are not? We begin by simply asking God to make us aware of his will for us. We ask for the willingness to trust God to inspire our thoughts and actions. Like the muscles in our body, we are free to exercise our will every day. Conforming our will to God's gives us the freedom to be who God intends us to be, rather than who others think we should be or who we think we should be for others.

Willingness to witness to the truth helps us to replace old fears and habits with trust in the Master's Plan. Think about how many times you've allowed old tapes to play in your head and talk you out of taking a risk, achieving a goal, or pursuing a dream. The truth is, our capacity to love, create, learn, and become our authentic selves, are so much greater if we are willing to believe in God's plan for us.

We must be willing to ask for help as we journey through life. It's a wonderful feeling when people seek us out and trust us with their stories. You are actually giving someone a gift when you ask him or her to receive your story. After all, relationships are built upon stories, those from ancient times and those from not so long ago. We all love a story, and the deeper and more real it is, the more empathetically we relate to it.

We see one man's willingness to persevere in faith in the scripture story of the man at the pool at Bethesda. One day, Jesus stopped at a healing pool where people gathered, hoping for a miraculous recovery from their illnesses. According to the story, the man lying by the pool had been ill for thirty-eight years. Jesus asked the man if he wanted to be well. Imagine you've been struggling with illness for thirty-eight years. What would your response be? I'm thinking I would say something like, "Are you kidding, me? Yes, yes! I want to be well; it's been thirty-eight years!"

This man tells Jesus that every time he gets close to the pool, someone cuts in front of him and he cannot get in. The man can barely move, so Jesus reaches out to him. Jesus tells him to pick up his sleeping mat and walk. When he obeys, the man is instantly cured and disappears into the crowd. Later, Jesus finds the man in the temple and tells him to go about his life, but to stop sinning.(John 5:1-9)

God beckons us to come just as we are, shortcomings and all. God asks us to be willing to do what it takes to be whole. Sometimes we want to be well, but we're not willing to do our part to get there. We want what we want when we want it! Faithfully, and despite all odds, we must be relentless in pursuing God's will for us.

We sometimes have little choice over our circumstances. However, we do have the choice to be happy. This is not necessarily the "throw your hands in the air" kind of happiness that is often fleeting. We want the inner peace and contentment that comes when we are willing to live in the present moment, regardless of what our circumstances happen to be. Circumstances are temporary and do not define us. Life throws us many curveballs. It doesn't always feel good. Our willingness to see things from a different perspective helps us redefine our happiness.

Be willing to notice what's really going on. Rather than labeling experiences as good or bad, begin to just notice how things are. Sometimes we build in automatic responses to things. This narrows our options each time we are called to respond, because we already have placed a judgment on it. For example, "I've given up on prayer, because every time I pray, nothing good seems to happen." There may be many reasons you feel this way. Explore those feelings. Rather than placing a judgment, open yourself up to the possibility of learning a new way to enter into prayer.

Ask for the willingness to right wrongs and make any necessary changes. If it's a long-standing resentment, you may want to ask for advice from a trusted mentor, member of the clergy, or friend. Whatever it takes to make restitution, we must be willing to do so, as long as it doesn't cause further pain and suffering. An outward apology, a letter, financial repayment, or changing our behavior are all ways to make up for a wrong. Every day, we must be willing to look at how our behaviors and words affect others in a negative way, and ask God to guide our hearts and minds toward change.

It's inevitable. We will stumble and fall, but when we are willing, the Spirit is there to guide us one baby step at a time. When we take it all to prayer, and ask for the willingness to start again, or to keep moving forward, or to be with whatever our present circumstances happen to be, we are accepting life as it comes to us. We cease trying to live in what could have been or what might be. It is in prayer that we talk with God about what we are noticing about our surroundings, actions, desires and thoughts. We ask to be aware of anything God wants us to do, think, see, or experience.

As the author Andre Gide once wrote, "One does not discover new lands without consenting to lose sight of the shore for a very long time." In order to grow, we must be willing to move into places that are quite unknown to us. Every day, we must rise asking God what it is we are to learn in this brand new day. And then we must open ourselves with complete willingness to accept it and learn from it.

PERSONAL REFLECTION

What does it mean to you to conform your will to God's?

When did self-will take you in a direction that was contrary to God's will? How did you come to that realization? What did you learn about yourself in this experience?

Describe an experience in which you became willing to allow God to guide and direct you? How did you feel?

What questions, thoughts, or reflections arise in you at this time?

Chapter 19

Openness

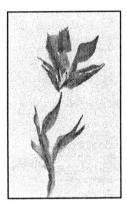

"Every human being on the face of the earth has a steel plate in his head, but if you lie down now and then and get as still as you can, it will slide open like elevator doors, letting in all the secret thoughts that have been standing around so patiently, pushing the button for a ride to the top. The real troubles in life happen when those doors stay closed for too long."
Sue Monk Kidd

Most couples experience periods during their marriage when the spark seems extinguished and one wonders if the light will ever come back on.

My husband and I were madly in love at the age of twenty-two. Two good people with promising careers, steady incomes, a healthy lifestyle, family support, and we shared common values and faith. What possibly could go wrong?

My husband and I did parenting pretty darn well. We didn't always do marriage so well. Issues with communication, intimacy, time management, and expectations plagued our marriage within ten years. Personal demons as well as the everyday stressors interfered with the work necessary to keep the flame alive. For me, the grass was looking greener on the other side. I was constantly comparing others' marriages to my own. The sacrament of marriage to which I committed entails sacrifice and unconditional love. It requires placing God at the center of the relationship. Honestly, I wanted God's help, but I didn't want to work that hard in my marriage.

One day, well into our marriage, we were driving north to visit our teenage boys at a summer camp. We finally had the courage to discuss divorce. I remember the heavy feeling in my chest, the intense sadness of that reality. Had it really come to this? After a while, we were both at a loss for words. The silence was crushing. We managed for our children's sakes to enjoy our time spent with them, but the drive home brought little resolution. Or did it?

We sought couples' counseling with little change. We then met with a couple from our parish that willingly spent countless hours listening and sharing their experiences and wisdom with us. Those were grace-filled hours. In the end, it was prayer that won the day. I remember turning my worries and desires over to God. I asked repeatedly for answers and guidance as to what I should do. I opened myself up to whatever it was that God thought was best. I asked God to remove my fears. No longer did I want to make a decision based on what others would think of me, or my own self-judgment; rather, I wanted to follow God's will. And every time I brought my prayer to God I felt him urging me to stay in my marriage. I kept hearing a small whisper inside that said, "I will be with you. Trust me." And so I did. It wasn't easy and there were times I slipped into self-doubt.

Within a few years my husband and I found ourselves refocused on shared goals and opportunities. A spark was rekindled and our marriage strengthened. We may have closed a door had we not been open to God's plan for our marriage.

Think of how many times you begin a thought, an idea, or have a desire, only to use the word "but" midway through it and slam the door on your possibilities. I would love to write poetry…but…I've always wanted to learn to play the piano…but… There is a quilt I want to attempt to sew…but…I'd like to volunteer at the soup kitchen…but… If we remain open to knowing God's will for us, our world broadens exponentially. God wants only the best for us, in a world where not everyone else does. When we keep an open mind and allow the Spirit to fill us up with new guidance or direction, rather than stale patterns and old ideas, we enter a world filled with new potential. To be truly open to God's message for us, we must resist the urge to make judgments about an experience before really taking it in and savoring the moments.

If opening ourselves up to God's plan reveals to us what we don't know, why is it so difficult for us to trust? Could it be, perhaps, that being open requires us to admit that we don't have all the answers?

If you've spent any time with a child between the ages of three and, let's say, ten years old, you've noticed they ask a lot of questions that mostly begin with "why?" They aren't afraid of looking stupid; their curiosity about everything is delightful—if not exhausting—to parents, at times. Somewhere along the line many of us begin to avoid asking questions. Perhaps we do not want to appear vulnerable, or to risk the possibility of judgment. It may be that we don't value others' suggestions as much as we do our own. Or it could be that we don't want to hear the answers given to us. Isn't that what strains relationships in families, in the workplace, on the practice fields, or between parents and teenagers—one or the other insists they know best?

Are you one of those people who think you have to have all the answers for everyone and every experience you encounter? It can be such a limiting pattern of behavior for us. It's not so much about feeling boastful of what we think we know, as much as being fearful that if we don't have the answers, others might think we are ignorant. We may be plagued by self-judgment that restricts our capacity to open ourselves up and to learn more.

There is a sense of freedom in saying "I don't know." The willingness to learn new things is truly a gift from God. What a wonderful feeling it is to open ourselves to whatever experiences God has in store for us. Living into our experiences rather than immediately judging them as good or bad opens the door of opportunity.

To achieve our full potential in our work relationships and our personal lives, we must be open to receiving God's gifts. In scripture, Paul writes a letter to the Romans in which he says, "God has given us different gifts for doing certain things well. So if God has given you the ability to prophesy, speak out with as much faith as God has given you. If your gift is serving others, serve them well. If you are a teacher, teach well. If your gift is to encourage others, be encouraging. If it is giving, give generously. If God has given you leadership ability, take the responsibility seriously. And if you have a gift for showing kindness to others, do it gladly. Don't just pretend to love others. Really love them."

Each and every one of us has been given gifts. The rich, the poor, the marginalized, the creative, the blue collar, the white collar, those with strong faith and those without, politicians and housewives, teachers and pupils, all races, creeds, and colors. Discover your gifts and be willing to open your heart and mind to the proper use of those gifts.

Keeping an open mind yields wonderful benefits:

- We begin to see our challenges as an opportunity for personal growth.
- It's perfectly acceptable to have our own opinion, but our worldview expands when we listen to others.
- Freeing ourselves of the need to control people, places, and things gives us a more peaceful inner life.
- Looking at something from a new perspective can bring positive change.
- Allowing yourself to become vulnerable gives others a chance to really get to know the authentic you.
- Failure is an opportunity to learn something new. It builds character and confidence.

Opening ourselves up to God's will enables us to see God's light, truth, and love. We can imagine ourselves as open vessels ready to receive whatever

God pours in. As the vessel fills, it yearns to spill its contents out into the world. If what spills out of us is of God, it is of love.

PERSONAL REFLECTION

What patterns, ideas, and expectations limit you from fully opening yourself up to knowing God's will for your life?

What areas of your life are calling for you to open yourself up to full capacity?

With whom or with what do you find yourself having the most negative judgments?
How would you want God's help with this? Explain.

What questions, thoughts, reflections arise in you at this time?

Chapter 20

Listening

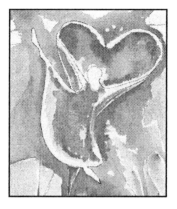

"Listening to God is at the heart of the gospel message."
Alice Fryling
"The Art of Spiritual Listening"

"God the Father said of Jesus, 'This is my Son, whom I love. Listen to him!'"
Mark 9:7

My youngest son was diagnosed with ADD in the second grade. At the time, I felt like the most inconsistent parent in the world. This child would give you the shirt off his back if you asked for it. He was loving, compassionate, and had a wonderful sense of humor. He was the kid in school that gravitated toward the classmate with a disability or the quiet one who didn't make friends easily. He also struggled with impulsivity and focus in school. At home, a timeout in his room could end up with mass destruction of property. I was hurt when I saw how peers sometimes reacted to him, although I understood it. His brother was often embarrassed by his behavior. It frequently disrupted the everyday flow of life in our household.

On one particular day, my son got into a pretty nasty fight while playing street hockey with neighborhood boys outside in the cul-de-sac. When I took him into the house, an angry battle of words ensued, followed by a temper tantrum and then quiet. We sat down together on our steps, totally exhausted and feeling helpless. With tears in my eyes, and seeing tears in his, I told my son I wasn't sure I knew how to help him. Keep in mind, this was supposedly my field of expertise, in nursing. At work, I dealt with children in far worse situations on a daily basis. Talk about feeling inadequate! He looked at me with a deep sadness in his eyes and told me he didn't know why he did the things he did, and that he wanted to "be like everyone else". It was a genuine moment for both of us. I was not just hearing words; I was listening with my heart. It was as if a light went on in my head. The message that I heard was the same message Mary received when she learned that she was carrying Jesus in her womb: "for nothing is impossible with God."

That very moment I prayed and asked God for help with my son. I so wanted to do the right thing, and was willing to do whatever it took to ensure as best I could that my child felt whole. A sense of peace came over me. I no longer felt alone with my concerns.

Within days, I spoke with the school counselor, a physician and therapist who offered guidance. My husband and I talked about ways we could better work together and share responsibilities with our son. We listened to our older son and began to help him find new ways to communicate with his brother.

This was far too personal. Sometimes we don't see or don't want to see what is right in front of us when we are so close to it. I had to give up thinking I knew what I really didn't know. Fear had been replaced by determination. Prayer replaced incessant worry. Trust in God led to new solutions.

There were several challenges to face at home as well as in school. As a family, we learned to pay attention to my son's words, body language, and actions. Listening required more than ears; it required open eyes, hearts, and minds.

Over the years, I've shared my story with parents. I remind them that one of the greatest gifts we can give to our children is to listen with an open mind and heart. It is only when we place our children and ourselves in God's hands and listen for guidance that we live freely and fully. Listening to God and those he placed in our lives for support does not mean that we are free of problems. Rather, with God's support, we can walk together through the problems.

Since we are not privy to the future, we must trust God with our present. My son went on to earn a BA in film production and his master's degree in theology. His work takes him all over the world, and, recently, he taught his mother how to bake the best loaf of bread ever! It's not surprising that he's been given the gift of becoming a wonderful listener.

My life's work as psychiatric and high school nurse, campus minister, spiritual director, and retreat leader has focused on listening. It was my role as mother that taught me one of my greatest lessons in listening. Another mother, Mary, the mother of Jesus, was my strength as I raised my children. How many times in our lives do we ask the question, "How can this be?" or "Why is this happening?" Mary asked those same questions when she learned she was pregnant. She listened to God, Joseph, the angel, and Elizabeth, and responded in faith and obedience to God.

The ministry of spiritual direction has taught me a great deal about the importance of listening. Hearing a story is one thing. Being able to hold another's experiences in sacred space is humbling. Day after day, we all meet people on their spiritual journeys. Some are willing to share their struggles with relationships and everyday life experiences with us. Whether they identify it or not, often people are trying to understand the role God is playing in their present experiences. As spiritual companions, we, along with God, tune into the person with whom we are journeying. In order for the Spirit to move through each of us, we must listen to what is said "between the lines." It helps to ask an open-ended question. This allows a person to go deeper into a place of wisdom and truth regarding their own circumstances. We are not the problem-solvers; rather we may be the conduit through which God speaks into the heart of each of us. Listening not only affords us an opportunity to empathize or understand another person, but to learn something more about ourselves.

Silence is important to the listening process. When we become quiet, our attention can be focused internally rather than on the external goings-on of our lives. In the silence, our minds can dream, hope, create, and be in touch with the movement of the spirit. Take a walk, a jog, or sit by a quiet flowing stream. Kneel in a place of worship or lie down under a shade tree and you will experience God's presence. The reason we say "silence is golden" is because it offers gifts far more important than all the wealth in the world. Our minds are freely open to receiving whatever it is God intends for us.

If someone is talking with you, pay attention. Have you ever been in a conversation with someone and all you are hearing is blah, blah, blah? Most often it's because our attention is either diverted or we're preoccupied by our own thoughts. Paying attention takes the focus from us and places it with the person to whom we are listening. If you're thinking about the next thing you want to say to the person, you're not paying attention. When our egos get the best of us, we begin to think more is better, when in fact, most often, the less we say with words, the better listeners we become.

Listening is a key component to good leadership. Whether leading a corporation or a Boy Scout troop, listening to those within the group and teaching others how to be better listeners is crucial to success. The high school leadership class I taught was full of exercises designed to help students listen to one another. Think about how often in the course of a day we interrupt another person who is talking. I am guilty of doing that. Being a good leader means we practice the skill of paying attention to the person speaking. We invite people into conversation as a way of allowing everyone the opportunity to share their thoughts. We manage a conversation so that one or two people in a group may not dominate the conversation. We allow spaces of time for silence.

Winston Churchill probably said it best: "Courage is what it takes to stand up and speak; courage is also what it takes to sit down and listen." I can get up in front of a group of people and say all kinds of wonderful and inspirational things. However, time spent listening and learning more about others humbles the soul.

Sometimes our own inner chatter drowns out the quiet whispers of the Spirit that lead us to a better understanding of God's will. It is in listening to our inner voice that we have a choice to act positively and effectually in our lives.

PERSONAL REFLECTION

If you were to rate your listening skills on a scale of 1-10 (10 being the best) where do you place yourself? Why? What needs your attention?

Describe a time when you listened with your heart. What did you notice about your reactions, your attitude, and your disposition?

Take five minutes and sit in silence. Describe what happened during and after that quiet time.

What questions, thoughts, reflections arise in you at this time?

Chapter 21

Hope

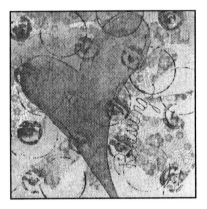

"The Lord is my inheritance; therefore, I will hope in him!"
Lamentations 3: 24

In spiritual direction, we become a companion to someone on his or her life journey. Along the journey, one begins to notice things about themselves, their relationship to others, and with God. At one time, I was working with a young woman in spiritual direction whom I will call Mary. Her husband returned from war after a year on the front lines of the battlefield. Mary described him as a very different man from the one that left her when his battalion left home a year earlier. His deep wounds were not physical, but mental and emotional. She was scared, lonely, sad, angry, and resentful because of her loss. Understanding that their relationship was forever changed, she initially felt a lot of raw emotion as well as a sense of hopelessness. The once warm and loving father seemed distant and preoccupied. The gregarious and energetic husband that left for war returned uncommunicative. Her gentle co-worker found it challenging to maintain solid relationships. The somewhat comfortable journey seemed to take a turn into the deep unknown, and Mary was feeling anything but sure-footed.

Over time, Mary allowed her wounds to be opened. She shared her deepest thoughts, feelings, and desires. Between sessions, she brought her everyday experiences to prayer. Slowly her anger turned into action. She began to advocate for her husband, her children, and other families suffering the often-silent pain of post -traumatic stress disorder. Loneliness fueled her desire to attend a support group aimed at helping her understand her husband's invisible wounds. Resentments motivated her to read and learn more about how to cope with the stressors. Hope began to bubble up in the midst of the turmoil. She was no longer feeling isolated.

She had breakthrough days and days that continued to challenge her, but she was beginning to experience what Sarah Ban Breathnach, in her book, Simple Abundance, describes as "divine discontent." English historian Dame Cicely Veronica Wedgwood describes this divine discontent beautifully: "discontent and disorder [are] signs of energy and hope, not of despair." Breathnach continues the thought by describing divine discontent as the "grit in the oyster before the pearl."

As an oyster grows in size, so must its shell. The oyster has an organ called a mantle that helps create the shell. The pearl begins to form when a foreign substance slips between the mantle and forming shell. The substance irritates the mantle and the oyster reacts by trying to cover up the irritant to protect itself; layer upon layer eventually forms the pearl.

Mary was certainly experiencing the painful irritants and grit of life's daily circumstances. At the same time, she was experiencing God amidst her suffering. She was beginning to see new possibilities ahead of her. She was able to mourn the passing of a life she once knew and move courageously with dignity and strength into a new period in her life. Leaning back into God's arms, she was willing to breathe and allow the Spirit to guide her through some very challenging days. Her pearl was being formed over time. She began to find her voice and acknowledge her talents. Mary was experiencing the capacity of her love to grow exponentially toward God, her family, and others.

She discovered that rather than trying to exert control and wasted worry *over her situation, she could rely on God to open her heart and mind to new possibilities. Mary would be the first to tell you her life isn't perfect. The wounds are healing with time and patience. Today she has a new outlook. She has hope for her future and the future of her family. She has discovered the pearl, the gift hidden in the discomfort of life's circumstances.*

We have all experienced feeling alone in our own pain. Many have experienced family suffering, broken marriages, children taking paths we wish they'd rather not go down, sickness and death, issues with lifelong friends or people we counted among our friends. We often have work-related anxieties, conflicts amidst our faith life, the burden of making everyday choices, or suffering losses and laments.

Hope is the universal force that motivates us to keep seeking solutions regardless of our present realities. It is about believing in possibilities. Our spiritual wealth is dependent on turning our lives over to the care of God. In Matthew's gospel, Jesus tells us, "Come to me, all you who are weary and carry heavy burdens, and I will give you rest… For my yoke fits perfectly, and the burden I give you is light." Living a mature spiritual life implies that we are willing to walk side by side and move in the direction God is taking us. Only then do we find rest and the ability to manage the distractions and burdens of daily life.

How can we be moved from a hopeless outlook toward one that renews us? Perhaps if we can muster the faith of a mustard seed, it is possible.

Begin with prayer. Open your heart and mind to the people, places, and experiences that allow you to receive the hope God desires for you. When we are experiencing hopelessness, we often find negative feelings buried inside of us. If, for example, we are angry with God, we may feel that our prayer is undesirable to him. If lonely, our prayer may feel desperate. Be assured that God can reach into our deepest hell and do for us that which we cannot do for ourselves. He listens to our prayers wherever and however we are. God desires our honest conversation with him.

Visualize a simple gesture or repeat an action that helps you to let go of anything that blocks you from feeling hopeful. A woman described a shaky relationship with God. She was unsure of how to approach God when she needed help. It came to her that by physically just leaning back a little she was able to visualize herself resting in God's loving arms. Whenever she needs reassurance, she relaxes her shoulders and purposely leans back a little as a reminder that God's got her back!

Use a chime on a watch or phone to ring every hour to remind you to pause and remember God's presence. A Catholic nun who teaches high school students said that upon hearing the church bells ring, she stops what she is doing and reminds herself to give thanks every hour. With the exception of your sleeping hours, you can find yourself remembering several times a day to pause and connect with God.

Visualize an empty bucket. When your bucket becomes filled with too much negativity, empty it completely, so that God can fill it with Living Water. Hope allows us to empty ourselves of negativity in order to let God reside in that space.

Think about the people in your life that have given you a glimmer of hope, those who believed in you when you might not have believed in yourself, or the ones who were willing to listen to your story no matter how many times you needed to repeat it. What about the people who offered you alterna-tives, not necessarily answers? Perhaps there were those who risked asking a question you may not have wanted to hear, but it helped you to go deeper. Hopeful people offer spiritual sustenance. They are willing to be vulnerable themselves. Like a cracked vessel, they have a light that shines despite their own imperfections and are eager to share this light with others.

Surround yourself with people who share positive energy. Ask yourself these questions: when someone meets me, do they see God in me? Do I resonate an inner light? We've all experienced those people that make us feel respected, worthy, and joyful. We too must make others feel important and special. Your words, your touch, and your presence may be someone's only brush with hope today.

Hope is a two-way street. Our mission from God is to receive this gift of light. We must then pour it out into the universe. Our day-to-day journeys will be met with life's frustrations, joys, and sorrows. It is when we accept our daily crosses and trust in God's plan that we live as hopeful people. If there is something we can give freely to the world that is more valuable than possessions, it is hope. We want to be the pearl, formed by all of life's grit, which becomes a beautiful gift to all who encounter us.

PERSONAL REFLECTION

Describe how life's grit is transforming you today.

What signs of hope are you experiencing these days? How are you a sign of hope for others?

Where are you feeling less than hopeful? Describe. How is God present to you in this experience? Explain.

What questions, thoughts, or reflections arise in you at this time?

Chapter 22

Loving

"If I love you, and I do, why would I plan for you a life that is joyless and loveless? It is my pleasure to bring you love."
Julia Cameron,
"Answered Prayers"

One day, while out on the playground at lunch, a kindergarten student hit a classmate in frustration. A teacher who witnessed the incident walked the student who committed the offense to the principal's office. The student sat in a chair in the waiting room as the teacher explained to the principal what had happened during the lunch recess. As this was his first time in the office, the student's anxiety and terror seemed almost more than he could bear.

My friend could hear the student's soft sniffles and nervous movements as he waited in her outer office. Finally, she asked the student to come in and have a seat, which was positioned directly in front of her desk. She asked him what happened to cause his now-visible tears. He looked up at her and began to explain what happened out on the playground. He stopped midsentence and his eyes began to circle around the room.

Located behind her desk, hanging in a window, was a decorative round prism. As a sunbeam hit the prism it began to reflect large, circular rainbows of light into the room. She watched as the boy's head bobbed up and down and all around until he finally asked in awe, "do you always get to work in the middle of rainbows?"

Totally disarmed by this simple observation, she smiled and responded that indeed her workday was filled with rainbows. After a brief discussion on better ways to handle his frustration, she walked the little boy back to his classroom.

A friend, who happens to be a school principal and spiritual director, shared this story that beautifully illustrates God's desire for us to be a loving light to others.

As I listened to my friend tell her heartwarming story, a deeper message began to resonate within me. In the midst of this child's angst and perhaps in her busyness, the light of love distracted both of them. The sight of rainbows seemingly appearing out of thin air temporarily soothed him. Anxiety and tension were replaced by wonder that rose up from deep within him. She was able to see beyond the mischief and into the child's heart. A skeptic might take the scientific point of view. Rainbows occur when light is being refracted as it moves through the faces of a prism. The cynic might see a child manipulating the conversation in order to avoid punishment. The spiritually minded person feels the movement of the Spirit and recognizes the gift of love hidden in an ordinary experience.

Wouldn't it be wonderful if in the midst of our ordinary moments we were able to experience the movements of God within them? It is awesome when we recognize the simple movement of love that emanates from our hearts to our minds and then is given expression in word, action, or thought.

Our definition of love and the capacity to love are always evolving. It is through life experiences that we gain wisdom and our understanding of love deepens. Think of a water balloon that is empty. It appears flaccid and shriveled with little capacity to hold much of anything. But as water is added, it stretches and becomes pliable so that it can withstand more water. It fills and eventually expands to a point that it can no longer contain the water and bursts open. While it is nearly impossible to be bursting at the seams at all times, we certainly can expand our capacity to love by allowing God to fill our hearts and minds with kindness, tolerance, compassion, patience, and all those things that are of love.

Love has this mushy, heart-shaped, candy-and-roses connotation in our society. As a Christian, my capacity to love is in direct proportion to my accepting the gift of the Cross. Surely the parent of a drug-addicted son or daughter, the child of a parent with dementia, the caretaker for hospice patients, or the teacher trying to reach a child who has given up, understands love as sacrifice. In his ministry, Jesus reached out to all those in need of healing. He spent time with the undesirables, poor, marginalized, and spiritually destitute. If we broaden our definition of poor, marginalized, and spiritually destitute, it becomes clear we are all in need of healing. Jesus' passion and agony was all about love, a selfless act, sacrifice, and willingness to do the Father's will.

Let's face it—we all have to admit there are days when even we are difficult to love. This is the point; it's easy to love lovable people. God needs us to go outside our comfort zone because our world is aching for more love.

The difficult-to-love are not hard to find. We see them or pass by them every day. Sometimes it's difficult to love the homeless person who hasn't showered in two weeks and holds a sign that reads, "will work for food". It's difficult to love the mother screaming at her child in the toy aisle at Walmart because the child wants to stop and play and she needs to get on with her business. Many times, the difficult-to-love are the people we work with who are demanding, family members who are angry and holding grudges, church members who hold different views than we do, teachers we think may be unfair, or politicians we feel are corrupt. The poor and marginalized, the prisoner, the peer who is different from us, the sick and elderly, the persons with mental health issues… all of these people we know in our communities, homes, schools, and churches are potentially difficult to love.

Loving is more than a response to a euphoric feeling. It is the act of letting go, the willingness to sacrifice and the ability to remain in the present no matter the circumstances. Love does not seek immediate answers to those things that cannot be explained. Rather, it faithfully waits. It is a willingness to choose kindness when faced by those who choose darkness. Someone's poor disposition, bad day, or unbearable attitude is an opportunity for us to shine our light into a dark space. True love says, "Come just as you are." It does not place personal expectations on others; rather, it accepts them where they are. We love by building up, not tearing down. I cannot love without joy in my heart. That joy comes from trusting God in all things.

I often imagine what it would have been like to sit with Jesus during those moments when he was "in such agony of spirit that his sweat fell to the ground like great drops of blood." (Lk 22:44) Not only was he feeling abandoned by those who loved him, but was agonizing over the impending death he knew he would suffer. And in those last moments alone, he showed his concern for us. "Holy Father, keep them and care for them-all those you have given me-so that they will be united just as we are." (Jn 17:11)

When we are lonely, afraid, overwhelmed, and feeling hopeless, we do have the opportunity to meet Jesus in the garden. He would stop everything and look into our eyes. He would take our hands in his and sit quietly and pray with us. All his energy would be focused on us despite his own desperate feelings. He would hold our pain in sacred space. Jesus says, "...I have revealed you to them and will keep on revealing you. I will do this so that your love for me may be in them and I in them." (Jn 17:26) This most human expression of Jesus' love and mercy is not only for us to witness, but also for us to experience as well in our own lives.

How many times have we told our children, "if you are in trouble, come and talk to us; there is nothing you could do or say that would make us love you any less." As parents, we mean those words with the deepest fiber of our being. We don't always like the choices our children make, but we love them totally and unconditionally. That is the way God pays attention to us. It is God's deepest pleasure to shower us with love.

Some say, if that is true, why do so many people suffer? Perhaps no one can adequately understand or give a sufficient answer to that question. It is a question that can only be answered in our personal way of faith. We do not see the big picture. Because we have been given free will, some people choose to hurt themselves or others. Sometimes it's not a choice at all; pain and suffering happen as the result of life's circumstances. God, who does understand the big picture, suffers with us, prays with us, and continuously offers us his love and support.

We are all called to love. Perhaps one of the most important questions posed in scripture by an expert in religious law was, "Teacher, what must I do to receive eternal life?" (Lk 10:25) Jesus didn't give an answer; instead he asked a question, "What does the law of Moses say? How do you read it?" (Lk 10:26)
Then the man answered, "You must love the Lord your God with all your heart, all your soul, all your strength, and all your mind."(Lk 10:27)

This doesn't leave much room for interpretation. Our hearts, minds, souls, and strength are pretty much everything about ourselves. It's our every breath, every muscle, thought, intuition, decision, prayer, and movement. And the second part of Jesus' statement is, "Love your neighbor as yourself." (Lk 10:27) We love ourselves by following God's will and becoming our most authentic selves. As we are becoming our authentic selves, our capacity to love and embrace all of God's universe expands. Sometimes to the point of bursting forth!

We are asked to love others completely as Jesus did and continues to do. We cannot do it alone. We would never have the strength and capacity to love the difficult-to-love if it were not for God inspiring us to open our hearts. Like Jesus, who asked the question, "How do you read it?" We too must ask ourselves the same question: what will it take for me to enter into eternal life with God? Listen for the answer. God is calling us to love. How and where am I called to respond? First, we need to pray for the willingness and then we need to act on it. We'll have plenty of opportunities to reach beyond our everyday experiences, and we need not compare ourselves to others. God calls us each in different ways to serve and love others.

PERSONAL REFLECTION

Do you believe God wants you to have a joyful and loving life? What makes you say yes or no?

When have you recently had an experience with a difficult-to-love person? What were the circumstances? How did you handle it? If you could change something about how you handled it, moving forward, what would that be?

"How do you read it?" What will it take for you to enter into eternal life?

List ten simple things you might do in order to expand your capacity to love. How will you put them into practice?

What questions, thoughts, reflections arise in you at this time?

Chapter 23

Forgiveness

"Forgiveness is the final form of love."
Reinhold Niebuhr

One of the most difficult experiences I had asking for forgiveness
came as the result of jealousy. I was an adult with children of my own,
which begged the question of who acted more childish, my children
or me?

I had a friend who was like a sister to me. A family moved in across
the street and this new mother befriended both my friend and I. At
some point I had it in my mind that this new gal was moving in a little
too much on the relationship I had with my friend.
As time went on, I found myself participating in gossip about this
neighbor. In particular I told an untruth about this woman, which put
her in a bad light with my friend. I was trying to make myself look
better by putting this other gal down.

Over time I began to see this gal for who she really was, a nice person
working hard to keep her family happy and content, working on her
spiritual life and struggling with the occasional self-doubts that we all

experience.

I felt the weight of my negative actions and reactions and began to understand that I needed to ask for forgiveness. I also knew I had to change my behavior. Making the decision to change my behavior was a matter of asking God to help me say and do the right thing no matter what was going on inside me. Somehow I had to right the wrong with regard to my part in the gossip and untruth I told about this neighbor. I could not approach her because she may have been unaware of the gossip. To retell it in front of her might give her more pain. What I needed to do was approach my friend and tell her that I had lied about our neighbor. That meant having to reveal a nasty side of myself that I'd rather she not know about. There was the fear that she might reject me or think poorly of me. Would our friendship be in jeopardy?

In the end, I sat down with my friend and admitted the whole truth. She appreciated my candor and it was never an issue between us. My attitude changed as I invited God into my circumstances.

That situation was one in which I owed the apology. Asking for forgiveness isn't always easy. Sometimes we repeat our offenses over and over. We find ourselves thinking, "Really? Is this happening again?" We feel guilty knowing that we're revisiting our shortcomings and once again asking for forgiveness. Faith reassures us that God hears and pardons our sin when we are willing to ask for forgiveness.

We are all broken in some ways. We seek healing in order to feel whole again. Giving and receiving forgiveness is essential to our maturing spiritual growth. When we experience the healing of wounds, we find inner peace.

We learn about forgiveness from the time we are tiny tots. Two toddlers are playing together in the sand box and one of them pulls the shovel out of the other's hand. Tears begin to fall. The mother of the tot now in possession of the shovel bends down to talk to her child. She tells him he must say he's sorry for taking the shovel and return it to his friend immediately. The impulsive child does as his mother asks. Tears dry up and the children continue to play.

That's the way we want our apologies to turn out. As we grow older, it gets more complicated. Learning to play together in the sandbox is a nice thought, but often we need more space and time. That space is in our hearts. Our capacity to forgive is in direct proportion to our willingness to invite God into the process. It could be that we are dragging our feet, but more often than not, we need time for prayer and reflection.

Many of us, too, understand the feeling of holding onto a grudge for way too long. We justify our anger by pointing the finger at the person whom we felt wronged us. We spend years paying the person back for the injustices we felt they perpetrated on those we love or ourselves. What we begin to realize is that over time our heart becomes weighed down with guilt and resentment usually long after the initial issues even came up.

Forgiveness does not mean that we excuse the person's behavior toward us. We recognize the unjust behavior and are willing to turn that person and ourselves over to God's care. We no longer have to carry or feed off the hurt. We no longer have to react to emotional baggage from the past. When negative feelings resurface, as they sometimes do, we focus on the present and keep our thoughts and desires centered in God's will. Sometimes it helps to repeat these words over and over again: "God, I give _____ to you."

This is a reminder that I am not in control, God is. I can choose not to react to another's words or actions. It is more important to maintain an inner calm.

There are volumes written on the topic of forgiveness. It is necessary to forgive and accept forgiveness in order for us to experience complete freedom in our lives. We can acquire wealth, security, status, popularity, and achievements, but if we are carrying around resentments and anger, we are not living in freedom. The same can be said if we are poor, insecure, unpopular, under-achieving, or living in a jail cell. If we cannot forgive or accept forgiveness, there is no inner freedom. No one is immune from experiencing bondage so long as we hold onto and allow those resentments to consume us.

Because we are called to love, ultimately, we are called to forgive. It is difficult to fully love and hold grudges and resentments against others at the same time. Forgiveness is a process. Sometimes our hearts have to writhe in pain, turn it over and over, and finally let the anguish go. Why? If we don't let go of the bitterness, we remain in bondage, in chains of our own discomfort. When we let go and let God take care of people that are either deserving or not of our forgiveness, we regain our sense of balance and self-respect. Physically, emotionally, and spiritually we can begin to heal from the inside out. God, who is love, is capable of giving us the strength to move forward and to live a joyous and free life.

Forgiveness, therefore, is our response to God's grace working inside of us. Are we willing to let go of what we are clinging to in order to let God fill us up inside? Are we willing to trade in our sorrow, discomfort, and anger for something unknown and new? Even when that unknown is better for us, we sometimes choose to stay with what we are sure of rather than to let go. Often, it's more about how we're feeling about ourselves than it is about the actual event or events that occurred to cause the anger and resentment.

The nature of forgiving is recognized within a snapshot of suffering. The snapshot is a moment in time. Whether perceived or real, people are hurting. Wounds may be resolved quickly or take years of healing. Comparing the feelings of those who lost loved ones at the hands of terrorists on September 11th to a disagreement between two friends caught up in a rift is a stretch, and yet, people are hurting and we are called to forgiveness in both circumstances.

A friend who lost his brother on September 11th in New York City put it this way: "On my own, I would never have been able to recognize the gifts that came out of my suffering. It was beyond my human capacity; it arrived by grace from a supernatural being whom I call God." He described to me the hatred he felt on September 12th and the process that brought him back to the teachings of his faith in a way he had never experienced previously.

After more than ten years, he has not attempted to understand why the terrorists did what they did. Rather, his willingness to forgive is based on the tenants of his faith. He believes that because of his faith in God, his prayer life, his understanding of the teachings of his spiritual ancestors and "many hours before the Eucharist," he is being freed from the chains of hatred.

In the process of forgiving, God gives us the gift of understanding others and ourselves better. God is capable of changing our hearts when nothing else in our own power seems to work. That is the key; it is our hearts we are allowing to be changed by God. We let go of bitterness and hatred not because someone else has changed, but because we seek to live in the light no matter what the choices of others.

My friend's loss, his pain and suffering, are deep. None of his memories of his brother can ever be forgotten or taken from him. Until he dies, it will always be a part of his story. What was perpetrated upon him and his family and the many families involved in losing someone they loved in the 9/11 attacks will never be forgotten. The acts themselves are unforgivable and vile. And yet, as radical as it sounds, we are called to forgiveness. Perhaps only by the grace of God can we come to a place of freedom in our hearts and minds.

Conversely, when we are the offender, we must come to recognize our part in the offense, admit it, and make a commitment to changing our behaviors so that we do not repeat the offense. Those involved in twelve-step programs understand forgiveness to be a re-occurring theme in the step process. Those in the Catholic faith are called to the sacrament of Reconciliation; in other words, making things right with God and those we've hurt. In most world religions, we see teachings that in some form or other deal with forgiveness. Saying we're sorry, like the little boy in the sandbox, is only one part of the process. We must find ways to right our wrongs.

There are some things to keep in mind as you prepare to make restitution to another person. Spend some time talking with God. Sincerely ask for help with the process. Be clear that by making amends you won't further injure anyone else in the process. Look only at your offenses; not the other person's offenses. Keep in mind that you are clearing up your insides. Whether your attempts to forgive are accepted by the other person or not is not your concern. Ask God for the willingness to follow through on any positive changes that need to be made in your behavior. Allow yourself to be led by the Spirit.

It was suggested to me by a spiritual advisor that in order to free our hearts and minds, we begin saying prayers for the person who needs forgiveness. Honestly, your initial intentions may feel insincere. We are encouraged to continue praying, no matter what we feel inside, because God can change our hearts. As we pray, we find ourselves asking God to help us move through the hurt and anger without acting out. We let go of expectations and completely turn our will over to God.

People often wonder how to make restitution to those who have died. Often rituals like letter writing, prayers, monetary and anonymous donations, or a commitment to a cause in the person's memory have served as ways to restore justice. Making changes in your actions and behaviors are a way to honor those in death.

Likewise, people often say the person we need to forgive most often is our self. A wise mentor once told me that if we are restoring balance in our own life by forgiving others and accepting forgiveness from others, we don't need to worry about ourselves. By our willingness to love and be loved, we will be at peace. We are actually experiencing the gift of forgiveness by living justly and rightly. We are experiencing an act of love when we are able to forgive and to accept forgiveness from others.

We usually find the most difficult persons to forgive are those whom we feel don't deserve our forgiveness. The psalmist writes, "[God] has not punished us for all our sins, nor does he deal with us as we deserve." God's unfailing love is far beyond our own; therefore, we must continue to ask for the grace and willingness to love others as we are loved.

PERSONAL REFLECTION

Is there something in your life that feels broken and is holding you back from living a completely free life? Describe.

Are you making attempts to seek or to offer forgiveness? Is there anything that stands in the way?

Have you attempted to take resentment against another person to God in prayer? Are you willing to pray for this person(s) daily? Can you imagine leaving this person in God's hands today?

Forgiveness

What questions, thoughts, reflections arise in you at this time?

Chapter 24

Empathy

"The friend who can be silent with us in a moment of despair or confusion, who can stay with us in an hour of grief and bereavement, who can tolerate not knowing, not curing, not healing and face with us the reality of our powerlessness, that is a friend who cares."
Henri J.M. Nouwen

Several years ago I taught a leadership course to high school juniors and seniors. One day, we had a school-wide assembly on the topics of respect and tolerance. At one point during the presentation, the guest speaker walked through the auditorium holding up shoes. As a sneaker, ballet slipper, and an athletic cleat were held high, he told the poignant stories he learned about the persons to whom the shoes belonged. He impressed upon the students that unless we've walked in someone else's shoes, what we see on the outside is not always the whole of someone's story.

It was a powerful presentation, and I wanted an opportunity to follow up with my students. I abandoned my planned lecture and immediately gathered my students in our group circle. This circle was usually reserved for the second half of the class as a sharing time for the group. I asked each student to remove one shoe and to place it in the center of the group circle. A few nervous giggles trickled out. I then asked each student to think about what their classmates might learn about them, if, for a day, those peers walked in their shoes.

One at a time, I invited students to retrieve their shoe from the center of the circle and share whatever it was they needed to share. There was complete silence in the group. I noticed some nervous movement. Some students looked straight down, some closed their eyes, and some had tears. I sensed they were uncomfortable with the silence. To rescue them by speaking would take away the power of the present opportunity, and so I held their anxiousness in the silence.

After ten minutes, the first young man expressed in a quivering voice his personal fears about leaving his family and hometown for college the following year. The floodgates were now open, and one by one each student shared a personal experience or feeling that he or she struggled with, unbeknownst to his or her peers. One student shared her sadness, fear, and anger over her father's recent death. Her suffering was palpable. A young man shared his fears about not always making healthy choices and instead following the crowd. Another spoke about feeling isolated from others, not feeling like he fit in.

As each student shared, it was apparent as they spoke, that their feelings and emotions were held in respect and confidence within the group. The Spirit moved within each one of us on that particular day. I didn't have to teach them lessons about empathy. They experienced it for each other. No one tried to fix anyone. Everyone seemed to listen with his or her heart. It was one of the most powerful classes we had as a group that semester.

🌾 🌾 🌾

As our spiritual lives mature, we understand empathy in terms of awareness of another's feelings and experiences. We don't necessarily understand exactly what a person is thinking or feeling or the reasons why, but we are willing to be present with them in their experience. The greatest gift we are able to offer those who are struggling is our willingness to listen and to be present. We are not there to give answers or fix problems, but rather to support and love the person going through whatever it is they are going through. I've come to understand that our opinions are far less valuable than opening our hearts to another who needs our support.

Think about it. People often ask us for our opinions. What they really want is to voice their feelings and to have someone really listen to them. People want to be heard. Next time someone asks your opinion, perhaps ask him or her a question. What is it that your heart desires? Tell me what you're thinking or what is it that you need from me? Asking an open-ended question allows a person to search his or her own heart. It is an opportunity to let them know you are listening and caring about what it is *they* think. You may be surprised to find that the person, because of your ability to listen, finds the answers within themselves. They'll be thanking you for all you did!

Our senses are the most powerful tools for experiencing empathy toward others. It's important to know how to use our senses for the optimum benefit of those in need. For example, silence is an important gift we extend to one another. Have you ever been with a small group of people, and someone is relating a difficult experience and begins to cry? Someone begins searching for tissues, another begins rubbing the person's shoulders, or someone interrupts to offer words of support. These actions, while well-intended, often change the dynamic of the moment. The person who is crying becomes distracted and the tears stop. More importantly the possible inner movement of feelings may be halted as well. Uninterrupted silence allows the person to fully express their deepest desires or feelings. True empathy allows the flow of feelings to be expressed while we are present to them.

Facial features are important. We need to be aware of making judgments with our eyes, forehead, and mouth. By relaxing and softening our features, we invite the person to feel safe in the sharing space.

Body posture speaks volumes. If sitting with another person, we want to make sure our chairs are at equal height. We don't want to be looking down upon the person who is sharing their thoughts and feelings with us. This

140

may inadvertently signal an imbalance of power or control. Sit comfortably without slouching. Being too relaxed may tell the other person we don't take what it is they are saying seriously. Give an adequate amount of space between you and the person you are speaking with. Sitting or standing too close may be intimidating, while standing too far away may make the person feel that we don't care.

If possible, try to find a space that is calm. If distractions are present, ask the person if perhaps they would like to move to a quieter area. Be careful not to make distractions a distraction. For example, if the person is talking, and a loud plane flies overhead, pointing it out may cause more distraction than just letting the person continue with their thoughts.

Of course, we will not always have the opportunity to control the environment in which we are communicating with another person. Awareness is key. A conscious connection with God is important when we are communicating with another person.

Walking in another's shoes doesn't mean we have lived the same experiences as that person. Because of our own experiences, values, and our own brokenness, we can relate to their struggles and hold their feelings in our heart. Are we able to hold another person's pain and allow them a safe place to share it?

It's not easy to stick around through someone's discomfort, as Ruth discovered. In the biblical book of Ruth, Naomi becomes a widow, experiences the death of her children, and severe poverty. She was feeling abandoned, angry, and full of sorrow. Think of how difficult it is to be around someone who is feeling so depressed. It would have been easy for her daughter-in-law Ruth to leave and return to her own family, but she decided to stay with Naomi. Together these women faced this rather hopeless situation.

Isn't it so true that during those times that we are at our lowest, God places someone in our life to bring us comfort and to reassure us that we are not alone? Like Naomi, who probably wondered why God abandoned her, we too know those who are tested by life's circumstances. Perhaps we will be the person like Ruth, whom God calls upon to help a friend, family member, or stranger, to remain focused on the important matters of life. Ruth wasn't called by God to solve the problems they faced together, but rather to be present with Naomi on the journey.

Empathy is the salve we can apply to open wounds when someone is at his or her most vulnerable. To experience someone's vulnerability is to allow them to expose their real selves bit by bit. It is a humbling experience that reaches beyond words. It's important to remember that empathy may not change the circumstances, but it allows a person to give voice to an experience in a safe space.

I believe God desires us to be his hands and feet on earth. Empathy towards another person is God showing up with *skin on* to be a companion to another person through a difficult circumstance or experience in their life. Simply, it is a willingness to be present and to hold another person right where they are. This is not necessarily a physical holding, but a spiritual and emotional holding. Ecclesiastes 4: 10 says it best. "If one person falls, the other can reach out and help. But people who are alone when they fall are in real trouble."

PERSONAL REFLECTION

Describe a time when you've experienced empathy from someone. What did he or she say or do or not do that comforted or strengthened you? What did the experience teach you about others and yourself?

Recall a time when you showed empathy toward another person. How did you express that feeling to them? Describe the feelings associated with this experience.

Is there someone in your life that you sense needs your empathy at this time? What might you do in the next few days to reach out to them?

What questions, thoughts or reflections arise in you at this time?

Chapter 25

Mindfulness

"Walk as if you are kissing the earth with your feet."
Thich Nhat Hanh

"I could see her coming toward me slowly. She was bent over her walker. The plastic bags hung off both sides of the walker, probably containing all her worldly possessions. My heart raced a bit. My step speeded up. I wanted to avoid eye contact; I was in a place foreign to me. And suddenly she spoke. She was asking for something; I had to look up. She smiled and reassured me she did not want money, just something to eat. I told her I had nothing...I was on my morning walk. She smiled and said, "you got a prayer for me then?" I placed my hands on her shoulders, smiled into those precious eyes, and assured her she would have my prayers. She disarmed me with her simple request. And when I thought I had nothing to offer, she made it possible.

Not more than a minute after speaking with the hungry woman, I was passing a church. I was going to keep walking, but noticed the sign with the daily mass schedule. Mass would begin in six minutes. I had prayers to offer. I had promised. I asked God for forgiveness—for apathy, avoidance, and omission. I prayed that the hungry lady would be fed and that all those who were hungry would find food this day.

I tried to avoid the face of God today and was given a second chance. I want to be mindful of how important a look, a touch, a smile, a connection, or a simple prayer can be to another human being. The next time God appears, will my eyes and heart be open?"

I had taken a walk in the early morning while visiting my son in Los Angeles. This was an excerpt from my journal.

We are not just made by God; we are made of God. "So God created people in his own image; God patterned them after himself; male and female he created them." (Genesis 1:27). How crazy is God about us, that he created us in his image and likeness from the mud of the earth? He breathed himself into us so that we can radiate God back out into the world.

Being mindful of the Creator keeps us grounded. The smaller we become, the greater God becomes. The greater God becomes, the more magnificent the universe appears to us. And when the universe appears magnificent to us, we can appreciate that we are walking on holy ground. We begin to treat everything and everyone in our path with respect and reverence.

Holy ground is any ground in which we are mindful of God's presence in the world. It can be the streets of our towns, our homes, places of worship, workplaces, schools, or someplace foreign to us. Wherever our feet trod is a place from which we may serve, honor, and praise God.

Mindfulness requires that we keep our feet planted firmly on the ground; in other words, we understand the "every-day-ness" of life to be a sacred gift. As our spiritual journey continues, we become more aware that everything begins and ends with God. We are connected to everything in the universe by the Master Builder's design. When we notice our interconnectedness, we become increasingly grateful, respectful, and aware of God's presence in our lives. We are more willing to remain in the present moment and appreciate its significance in the unfolding story that is our life. This is not always an easy thing to do, given our busy schedules and the constant distractions in our daily life. For many, remaining in the moment takes focus and practice. Our inclination, especially when the present moment feels unpleasant, is to relive the past or jump into the future.

To be mindful is to be aware of the presence of God within us and around us. We do this intentionally. Simply, we become an observer of what we are feeling and how we are responding to everything and everyone we come in contact with in our world. We become aware of choices and mull them over. Before acting on them, we simply place them in sacred trust. Together with God we proceed. Sometimes this becomes second nature to us and sometimes we have to work at it. We can improve our ability to pay attention to how we are feeling and responding to stimuli.

Remaining mindful involves very simple practices:

- Stay in the day! Ask God to help you remain focused on the now of life.

- Be aware of your abundance and thank God every day for whatever gifts, expected or unexpected, come your way.

- Sometimes, God is the only one who sees the "big picture." Trust God to reveal it in his own time.

- Open yourself to the movement of the Spirit. Trust your gut instincts and intuitions to God's whim.

- Live into your prayer life. Allow ordinary tasks to honor, serve, and praise God.

- Take time for quiet meditation, to read scripture, or inspirational materials. Focusing on a word, phrase, or mantra helps you to remain centered in God.

- Be intentional about service. Do something small every day for someone and seek no recognition. Rather, thank God for the opportunity to make someone happy or to lighten a load.

- Empty yourself of useless worry. Declutter your personal space.

Make it easier for God to enter in and create sacred space within and around you.

- Pay attention to how you speak to others. What does your voice sound like? How do you let people know what you need? How do people respond to you? Do you really listen to others or are you trying to think of how to respond to them?

- Notice the natural world around you. Make small changes that help you to care for the earth and all creatures.

- Live with the questions. God, in time, will make known what needs to be made known. Don't fret about things you cannot change. Give it all to God. Find peace in the Divine One.

PERSONAL REFLECTION

Take a few moments to be aware of the space in which your feet are "kissing the earth". Gently remind yourself of how closely you are connected to the earth. What are you mindful of as you take this posture?

Think of ways you may become more mindful of God's presence in your day.

What questions, thoughts, reflections arise in you at this time?

Chapter 26

Generosity

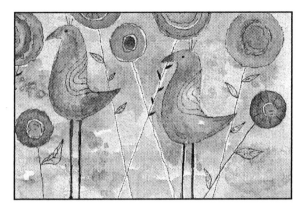

*"Successful people live well, laugh often, and love much.
They've filled a niche and accomplished tasks so as to leave the
world better than they found it, while looking for the best in
others and giving the best they have."*
Ralph Waldo Emerson

*I met Father Marc when we were stationed in Kodiak, Alaska. He was
the pastor of our chapel on the Coast Guard base. A couple years later,
he resigned his military commission. As a comfortable and successful
career ended, he answered God's call to work in Haiti amidst some of
the poorest conditions in the world. He sold all his belongings in the
states and traveled to Port-au-Prince with a blessing from his order
and little else.*

*Initially given a small run-down house, he took in orphan boys from
the streets to feed and teach them. The number of children seeking
his care and compassion grew. Father Marc saved enough money
through generous donations from family and friends to purchase
land in the southwest part of the country. Soon he was building small
cement houses on the property and employing a staff to care for the*

children. He oversaw the building of two schools, a small medical clinic, and dining hall that provided basic care and nourishment for the burgeoning number of orphaned and poor children. A small village arose. Building and agriculture programs were put in place to teach the older children skills necessary for making a living.

Over six hundred children a day now receive physical, emotional, and spiritual nourishment from this man they call Papa. Father Marc calls this place holy ground. It is where he meets God face-to-face on a daily basis. When he leaves the island periodically to raise money and awareness in the churches and communities of the U.S., the children plead with him, "Papa, don't forget us." And he never does. He would tell you he's been tested more times than he can count. He trusts God to provide generous people to help him feed, clothe, and teach these children. For many of us, we cannot imagine choosing to live our life among the poorest of the poor. Father Marc answered his call from God.

Perhaps we aren't called to leave this country, sell all our belongings, and live amongst the poor like Father Marc or Mother Teresa. Certainly, we are called by God to live with the heart of a servant. Scriptures tell us that we don't live lives in order to make a good impression on others, but to humble ourselves and treat others with love, respect, and compassion. Sacrifice and suffering may be a part of our work on earth.

We admire the generous spirit of those who care for the marginalized of the world. They are people who give without attachment to their gift. If we're honest, this is very difficult to do. At some level many of us continue to seek recognition for the gifts we give to others. While it feels good to be recognized, we may want to continue to pray for being detached from any kind of personal expectation or reward. Our desire for a generous spirit of giving, purely motivated by God's will that it be done, and nothing else, is reward enough.

Generosity is a state of the heart and mind. It is a place from which you are filled with grace and blessings, with a willingness to give freely and think about others' needs. Some generous people have great riches and wealth, while others have no money and few possessions. Generosity is not about the things we have; rather, it is about what we are willing to give despite the things we have. Coming to understand our gifts and how to use them to benefit others is really the key to our inner joy.

Whether we realize it or not, God works through us to reach people he thinks need us. Have you ever shared an experience with someone only to find out some time later that your story gave them strength and hope? Without being aware of it, our words and actions affect others. If we possess a generous spirit, those words and actions can impact people around us in a positive way, without our ever realizing the extent of it.

Remember back to a Christmas when you searched for the perfect gift for someone you loved. Perhaps, you searched high and low until you found that special something or maybe you created something personal with your own talents. The excitement and anticipation of giving this gift and seeing the person you love open it was far more important than getting something in return. When we give from the heart, the reward is internal. Generosity allows us to transcend our own pettiness.

Recognizing gifts from others is an important aspect of a generous spirit. Not only physical gifts, but those that come in the form of life lessons. When we are able to receive whatever it is God wants us to learn, our minds are open to greater possibilities.

Generosity begins in our homes and with our families and friends. Spending time with an aging parent, reading a book to your child, listening to a neighbor share a vulnerable moment, taking time to share your creativity, and serving those less fortunate are opportunities to give generously of our time, talent, and treasure.

Sometimes, it is when we feel uninspired that giving of ourselves becomes a gift that unintentionally reenergizes us. Generosity is selfless and inspired by God's grace. It seeks no return. It may require sacrifice. It often takes us out of our own comfort zone. Generosity is born of love. Being filled with a generous spirit creates a positive energy. God delights in us and that energy moves from person to person and lives are changed. The effort can be very simple. If we look in our own backyard, we will always find someone who may benefit from our kindness and generosity in each day.

To open yourself to becoming a more generous person, it often helps to pray and ask God to help you notice opportunities where your gifts and talents can be used to help others. If you are tempted to think, "I don't have anything I can offer," stop and redirect your thoughts toward God and out into this vast universe. Remain positive and open. Opportunities will be abundant.

Ask God to remove fears that incapacitate you from taking actions that the Spirit intends for you. Ask him to remove your fear of lack so that your heart will serve willingly, to remove your fear of monetary loss, and to take away intolerance. You may petition God's help in stripping you of pride and self-centeredness, or allowing you to step into another's shoes before you pass judgment. Surrender your egotism to God so that you become willing to do even the most mundane of services without seeking recognition.

Finally, avoid placing negative judgments on generous actions or deeds; for example, "this isn't enough" or " what will this matter?" If the Spirit moves you to act generously, simply thank God.

PERSONAL REFLECTION

What do you have to offer in the way of time, talent, or treasure? How are you using your gifts with a generous spirit?

Describe a time when the recipient has repaid your generosity. How did it make you feel?

Whom do you look to as a role model for generosity? Why?

Have you found your niche? That wonderful place where you feel called by God to practice charity and give abundantly of yourself so that others benefit from your gifts? There are many niches along our journey that potentially can be filled.

What questions, thoughts, reflections arise in you at this time?

Chapter 27

Patience

"Be patient toward all that is unsolved in your heart and try to love the questions themselves, like locked rooms and like books that are now written in a very foreign tongue. Do not now seek answers, which cannot be given you because you would not be able to live them. And the point is, to live everything. Live the questions now. Perhaps you will then gradually, without noticing it, live along some distant day into the answers."
Rainer Maria Rilke

One day, for my morning jog, I decided to take a route that ended with a formidable hill almost a mile in distance. As I rounded the last corner and began my ascent, I questioned how I could have possibly made this choice. I wanted to turn back and avoid the hill, not wanting to experience the stress on my body, the mind games that surely would ensue and the shortness of breath.

Suddenly, I felt the presence of the Holy Spirit. A whisper deep from within quieted my mind. Instead of thinking of how I would make it to the top of the hill, I was focused on the space right beneath my feet. One step at a time, I breathed into that space. Rather than looking up and ahead, I fixed my eyes on the road right before me. The rhythm of each step carried me forward and before I knew it I had conquered that seemingly insurmountable hill.

It's quite simple. I do not enjoy waiting — for my car to be repaired, for people who are late, to be given long and tedious directions or for results of any kind. Most often, it's not the big things that drive me crazy. I usually recognize when something is too big to handle or too far out of my control. It is the day-to-day habitual experiences that can catch me off guard and send me into a "tizzy-fit" when they don't go as I had planned.

I compare patience to a strenuous workout. I don't necessarily enjoy the process but love the results.

My recovery from food addiction has helped me to better understand the importance of letting a process unfold in God's time and with his guidance. Many unforeseen gifts have been wrought through this experience. It has been nothing close to perfect. Just as in life, there is a rhythm to recovery. Initially, it was easy to become discouraged that things weren't happening quickly enough. With the support of others, I began to understand that sometimes it was going to feel as though I was trudging uphill. There were always reminders to focus on one step at a time.

There were periods in recovery when I would reach a plateau and not much seemed to change. I could feel myself getting restless. I felt like there was something I could be doing but I wasn't sure what it was. Since I was used to living at extremes, just "being" initially felt disconcerting. There were valleys as well, periods where my energy and creativity were quite low. Sometimes, I felt like I was in a desert, dry and parched, waiting desperately for something to shift or move. Over time I realized this was a period intended for rest and renewal, a time to catch my breath and wait for the Spirit to move me wherever I was meant to go.

I can attest that waiting on God's timetable is not always easy. Going deeper, discovering life's rhythms, acquiring experiences, creating balance and a sense of well-being is the treasure unearthed by cultivating patience.

Writing this book has taught me a lot about patience. Sometimes I felt inspired; words and ideas were tumbling to the page. Other times, the well seemed dry and nothing came together. When I felt stuck, rather than panic, I prayed for the willingness to keep moving forward. For an entire year, I practiced writing reflections once a day. I carried a pen and paper with me everywhere I went. If an inspirational thought surfaced, I would write it down. A friend called this the period of the "Divinely Inspired Note-taker." The book was on hold while I was learning more about the writing process.

Gradually I was inspired to write for longer periods of time. There were plenty of obstacles but somehow I trusted they would be handled in due time. There was no magic pill I could take to turn the energy and creativity back on. I needed to be patient and to continue doing whatever I could to keep the process alive. Waiting is not easy for a self-confessed control freak! But, no amount of worry was going to change things. Rather than give up on the writing, I kept an open heart and mind, reaching toward every possible opportunity available. I know today that no time was wasted in this process. The practice reflections helped build my confidence. The times when I felt uninspired were just periods of re-energizing and learning.

What makes you impatient? Who are the people, what types of events and circumstances, trigger you to feel impatient? For many of us, it is our expectations that inevitably create inner distress. The delivery is late, something we count on to work breaks down, someone is not meeting our expectations, and the schedule is too slow or too hurried. If you don't see immediate results, do you panic? Do you expect only perfection from yourself, from others? When the result isn't perfect, do you begin to beat up on yourself emotionally? Are you a list-maker and tight schedule-keeper? What happens when a kink is thrown into your best-laid plans? Awareness of what makes us impatient helps us to better understand and prepare ourselves to respond more appropriately when we find ourselves becoming unglued.

How do we learn to grow our patience?

The biggest stumbling block to our patience is the temptation to look for a quick-fix solution to our problems. Balance is possible only when we remain connected to God's plan for us. As we journey on our spiritual path, we need to resist the shortcuts that can sidetrack us from realizing the authentic person God calls us to be.

Be aware of your natural responses to daily life. How do you respond to both the slightest and most challenging stresses? What physical changes do you notice in your body? Do you notice your shoulders or hands tensing up? Some people talk too much while others can't find the words to speak. Does your heart beat faster? Are you shaking your foot or wringing your hands? Mentally, do you become overwhelmed, as your mind begins to race with many thoughts? Do you begin to formulate new plans or perseverate on past ideas? Are you grateful for what is or easily upset by what is not? Do you adapt easily to change or do you have difficulty with it? Spiritually, do you curse or pray more readily when an uncomfortable situation arises? Do you ask for help and trust God's timetable?

Notice the patterns that form in response to people, places, and things that try every last nerve in your body. Assess your responses to changes and circumstances in your everyday life. Are your habitual responses causing positive or negative energy toward yourself and others? It is only by noticing these patterns in our behavior that we can then make changes, if necessary.

If something in your life seems to be bringing up more questions than answers, if someone or something has you frustrated and losing patience, take a deep breath and calm your body. We want to respond to life from a place of inner calm and thoughtfulness.

Try to avoid triggers that cause you to lose your patience. Walk away. For me, when the inspiration felt low or I had spent enough time writing at the computer, I would take a break and do something simple or relaxing. Taking a break from whatever causes you to get into a tailspin is a great way to decompress and let go of building tension.

Time is our friend. It helps give us a fresh perspective, renews our energy, allows for prayer and discernment, and gives us opportunities to reflect on healthy choices.

Reflect on what really matters in your life. Think of how often we get "bent out of shape" over the littlest things. Keep your focus on who God is calling you to be. If your actions are honoring, serving, and praising God, that's what really matters.

Find positive stress relievers. Read, pray, walk, exercise. Write in a journal; sit and talk with a spiritual director or trusted friend about things that may be causing you to lose your cool. Caring for yourself improves your ability to remain calm, balanced, and patient.

Check your attitude! If people seem to be causing you distress more often, look first at yourself. Have you been a willing listener? Are you open to others' opinions? Have you been tolerant and compassionate toward others? Have your expectations been excessive or nonexistent? Are you easily distracted or sidetracked by issues and concerns that could be clouding your judgment? Be aware of how your attitude is affecting outcomes. Perhaps it's time for changes.

Although we're still not as patient as we'd like to be with others, and ourselves, perhaps, we are learning not to take ourselves quite so seriously. Relax and take that first deep cleansing breath and think before you speak. The world will not end because something doesn't go our way. Just breathe.

PERSONAL REFLECTION

When was the last time you felt yourself being impatient? What did it look like? Describe how it felt inside.

What works to help calm you? Is there anything you might want to consider that would help you to recognize your impatience, and help you deal with it more effectively? Describe.

Explain how God is patient with you. What are the signs that let you know God is present in situations that require your patience?

What questions, thoughts, reflections arise in you at this time?

Chapter 28

Presence

" The most precious gift we can offer others is our presence.
When mindfulness embraces those we love,
they will bloom like flowers."

Thich Nhat Hanh

I sat in an inner city bus/train station for two and a half hours waiting on a train that would take me to my comfortable home. It was rainy, cold, and damp outside. Inside, I watched children play as drug dealers pushed their poison. Homeless men and women with sores on their bodies tried to find a comfortable place to rest. Some laid on heating vents to stay warm. The mentally ill hallucinated and conversed with no one in particular. Some looked hungry. Others appeared cold. Sad and distant eyes appeared hopeless and begged for recognition.

From my seat on the floor, I watched this seemingly routine scene unfold. I felt extremely uncomfortable, even fearful at times. I thought to myself, "I do not know this world they live in, yet I'm a part of it. This is my world." I've volunteered in soup kitchens and prisons, but this was different. There were no boundaries in this place, no familiar faces, no one to answer questions or give guidance. This experience was real and raw. I was alone and definitely out of my comfort zone.

Several persons caught my attention, and I began to wonder about their lives, their struggles, and their dreams. Questions floated in my head; did they experience loving relationships? Was a nutritious meal available to them this day? Did they have meaningful work? Did they feel safe when they returned home, or were the streets their home?

I silently began to pray: "God, I have no gift to offer." I asked that any intolerance, judgment, or cynicism be removed. My mind and heart began to soften. The fear melted into awareness. I heard God silently speak these words: "Do. Not. Look. Away." I found myself letting my eyes meet theirs and offered a smile to those who passed me by. I played with a few of the children close by. Compassion, dignity, and a silent prayer of hope were all I had to offer.

God reminded me that the gift I could offer was, simply, presence. Sadly, so often, my time, treasure, and talent are offered out of a sense of obligation rather than from a place of humility. So many times there are strings attached in some way. This day, although a small offering, it was sincere and from the heart.

By placing God in the center of my world, every thought and action was an extension of God inside of me, simply being present to the world of which I am a part.

How many times have we begun a thought by saying something like, "when I get that job…," "when I make enough money…," "when I lose weight…," "if my kids would only…," "when things slow down…," "when my boss…," "when the weather improves…," " if I feel like it…," "when they apologize?"

When and if can become excuses to put our lives on hold and to cast off the present for some unforeseen, ideal "someday." Problem is, we keep putting off and putting off and someday never seems to come. Presence is about accepting life just as it is— warts and all. We don't have to like it, but to really live in the moment, we must be paying attention to whatever our reality is. It is remaining *focused in*, with your whole being, upon that which is immediately in front of you.

Presence is pure. It is intentionally being with someone or something without expecting anything in return. It is simply *being* in the moment. And when we open ourselves to the Great Unknown and become a vessel to receive grace, opportunities unfold. Rather than trying to force our will upon life, when we empty ourselves and let the vessel be filled with the Spirit's intentions for us, we are filled. As we feel the movement of the Spirit, we can choose to act upon our intentions or not; the choice is ours.

Pausing and noticing what is happening in the natural world around us is a way of being present to life. Our senses give us an opportunity to drink in the beauty of God's creation. Sometimes we become preoccupied with future events and we don't take time to stop and pay attention to what the natural world is teaching us. Look to the buds on the trees, the ocean waves crashing to shore, the singing of birds or restlessness of the wind to teach you about God's timetable. The natural world unfolds with perfect timing. Spend time with your feet planted firmly on the ground. The closer you are connected with the natural rhythm of life, the more truly present you will be to yourself, God, and others.

I had an experience one early spring day while on a retreat that brought home the idea of presence. I joined eight lovely women, whom I did not know, at a seaside retreat center. I went with the intent of leaving all my work behind for the one-day retreat. I purposely did not bring a computer, phone, book, journal, or even a pen. I wanted to let the Spirit move me wherever it wanted to take me.

It was a bit windy, and a cold, damp drizzle fell throughout the day. The sky and the ocean water blended together in a steely gray color. Despite the chill in the air, I had always been drawn to this secluded beach for walks and thoughtful reflection. This day was no different.

After Morning Prayer and reflection, the retreat leader played a musical meditation. She told us that upon completion of the meditation, we were invited to spend time with God, however we were moved to do so. Part of my desire for this retreat day was to take a walk on the beach. The weather certainly wasn't cooperating as I had wished.

As the music played, a thought kept popping into my head: "I don't want my hair to get messed up in the wind and rain." I was totally distracted by the idea that I might look like a drowned rat should I follow my desire to walk on the beach this particular morning.

I remembered hearing someone say that we have five seconds to make a decision about an internal desire before our brains begin to reason or talk us out of it. Sometimes that's a necessary thing, but sometimes, we ignore our deepest God-driven desires just to "keep it safe." After four seconds, I got up from my chair and walked outside toward the beach, leaving my concerns about my hair aside. After a long walk at the beach, I began my journey back to the center.

I noticed crocuses and daffodils, some budding and a few blooming. There was a pussy willow bush with branches so long and full, they were drooping towards the ground. Patches of spring grass grew in the safely protected spots and trees were filled with buds still wrapped tightly in themselves.

I thought to myself, *nature doesn't need to respond to the five-second rule.* A tree is just a tree. It waits patiently for its time to bloom. The daffodils wait for the ground to thaw, the warming of the sun, greater length of light, and for spring rains to quench their thirst. Perhaps they respond to the gentle hands of the gardener who delicately nurtures the soil.

We have the privilege of choice. We can choose to follow God's desire for us or not. We can engage in life's musings or not. The natural world invites us to play; we have the choice to engage or not. We have the freedom to be our true selves or not.

We certainly can take a few lessons from the trees and daffodils and the rhythm of the seasons. We are called to be just who we are. God doesn't love us once we are who we think we should be; God loves us right where we are, warts and all. Think about how wonderful it is when we bloom in God's time and allow ourselves to be nurtured by the Beloved.

How truly grateful I was on that day to remember the five-second rule and to follow the Spirit's whimsical invitation to play and remain present to the moment. How blessed it felt to remain in God's presence. I had other choices. I could have played it safe.

When we consciously invite God into the space we share with others, it is more likely that we will remain open to what it is we need to say or do. For example, someone may share his or her feelings of loss with us. God can help us find simple words that may be consoling. Perhaps words are unnecessary, and instead we are moved to rest a hand on his or her shoulder. Trusting God, we are guided to speak or act as he inspires us to do. We intentionally remain focused in the moment.

Presence takes practice. We live in a world where we can be visually, verbally, and virtually bombarded to the point of total distraction twenty-four hours a day. Whether we are working, vacationing, praying, parenting, or living out our vocations, we must place God at our center or we risk being distracted by things that take us away from what really matters in life. Expectations often get in the way of our ability to be present to a person, event, or opportunity. Expectations can be distractions that keep our focus elsewhere.

Looking forward is not a bad thing so long as we aren't ignoring or somehow trying to avoid our present circumstances. Presence requires a willingness to remain focused in the "nowness" of our days. By opening ourselves to God's grace, we receive the invitation to explore new opportunities as we journey through each day. Remaining present takes me out of my selfishness and humbles me to a Greater Plan.

As we give our time, talents, and treasures to others, let us be reminded that presence is often the greatest gift we can give another person. As God is present to us, so God asks us to be a presence to those who journey with us as well as those whose paths we cross either by design or serendipity.

PERSONAL REFLECTION

Describe *presence* in your own words. Recall a time in which you were *focused in* with your whole being to another. Describe what that felt like for you.

What distractions keep you from being totally present to another?

Estimate how many minutes during the waking hours of a day you take to be present to God. Do you feel it is enough for you? Why or why not?

What questions, thoughts, reflections arise in you at this time?

Chapter 29

Gratitude

"Praise the bridge that carried you over."
George Colman

I am most grateful for friendships that have become part of the fabric of my life. One such person is a friend I met while in high school. This friendship didn't start up in a classroom, in the cafeteria, or in the halls of the high school, but rather in the gym, at a basketball game.

He came to my hometown from New York City in 1912, when he was twelve years old. He worked on the family farm on the outskirts of town his entire life. We were both seniors, I in high school, and he seasoned with wisdom.

Apparently he loved watching sports and regularly attended the girls' basketball games at the high school. One day, as I was waiting for my sister's game to begin, an older gentleman approached and asked if I had a winter sports schedule handy. I told him I did not, but would be glad to pick one up for him and bring it to the next home game. It would have been easy to blow off this request; however, there was something about this gentle man I could not forget.

The following day I remembered this yet-nameless man's request and retrieved a schedule from the main office. I carried it with me to the next game.

As I saw the older gentleman come into the high school gym, I ran down the bleacher steps, pulled the schedule from my pocket, and sat down beside him. We introduced ourselves to one another. His name was Arthur, though most everyone called him Art. We made small talk about the upcoming season, and after our conversation, I returned to my seat. A quick wave good-bye at the end of the game and our brief encounter seemed like history.

Later, Arthur sent me a beautiful note thanking me for remembering to bring the sports schedule. To me, the simple act of retrieving a schedule certainly didn't warrant such a response. To Arthur, any act of kindness was an opportunity for him to express his gratitude.

I was touched by his response. I made it a point to spend a little time with Arthur before every game he attended. We talked about family, the farm, his love of gardening, his childhood or whatever!

Our friendship grew over the years. Every summer I received complimentary tickets to the hometown fair. Arthur was so proud of his flower arrangements and decorated gourds. He created mobiles of his "famous friends"; pictures of movie stars with the name of locals whom he thought resembled the star. One summer he proudly showed me that my name had been added to his mobile. Invitations to the farm for an ice cream social and tour of the gardens were answered enthusiastically. I wasn't the only person whose life was touched by this gracious man, although he had a way of making each person feel like the most special friend in the world.

Letters and cards went both ways through college and after I moved away. Birthday greetings, graduation cards, letters of support, updates, pictures, and articles cut from the local paper went back and forth for many years, until at last Arthur could no longer write.

Arthur taught me a lot about gratitude. Although we never talked about it, I knew he was a spiritual man. He reveled in the beauty of nature and loved the land he farmed. He treated everyone he met with respect and dignity. He was a master in the art of "joy-making" and of giving thanks. Arthur showed me that it is in simplicity that we find our most treasured gifts. And the gifts we receive, no matter how simple, can be re-gifted to others.

Ultimately, we spend our entire lives discovering and learning to embrace the gifts of the Beloved Gift-giver. The first gift we receive even before being gifted to our parents at birth is the promise from God that we will not journey alone. Imagine the hand of God caressing and holding you in the womb of your mother. God speaks to you through the words of the prophet Isaiah, "I would not forget you! I have written your name on my hand." (Isaiah 49:16) God promises to be with us through life's joys and trials. He places people in our lives that will teach us, guide us, nurture us, and love us into our authentic selves. What greater gift than to be molded into the person God intends for us to be?

We are given the gifts of body, mind, and soul. We have brains to think, process, create, and make decisions. The Creator makes possible our relationships, accomplishments, and experiences. The natural world provides a rich canopy upon which we play, rest, recreate, and build dreams. We cannot claim anything as our own. It is all gift.

As we begin to unearth and discover our gifts in the very ordinary experiences of daily life, we can't help but give praise to the Gift-giver. We cultivate gratitude by accepting these gifts and what is before us, trusting God's presence in them.

A prayer of thanks is often the simplest form of gratitude. "Thank You, God," goes a long way toward recognizing the Creator of all goodness. A flower responds to the light by opening itself up. By noticing the simple and often natural gifts in our day, we cultivate a gracious heart.

We begin to open ourselves to the opportunities that are before us. In time, as our spiritual lives mature, we come to realize that gifts are often buried in our trials. Sometimes, in order to discover and embrace the gifts God intends for us, we must slog through the muck. Surely, those experiencing loss, addiction, or anger may not immediately see a gift within the experience. Moments of difficulty and pain may render us temporarily blind to the gifts of the Spirit, and thus we do not see the larger picture. We may not understand the gift until time allows us to heal, move forward, or gain strength.

Like roots that firmly take hold below the surface of the soil, we must firmly let our roots take hold in God. A flowering seed doesn't remain dormant. It receives the rain droplets, the sunshine, and the nutrients from the soil. It grows, blooms, and spreads its roots. It needs nothing more than to receive what God intends for it in order to grow. We, too, must receive what it is that God intends for us. Gratitude and appreciation grow from noticing our abundance.

Gratitude for the things of life is a temporary state. We are grateful for the shiny new convertible, buying a new house, being given new ring or inheriting a vacation home. Studies show that no matter what our experiences, when it comes to new things, they affect us usually for only a short period of time. When we truly take time to think about what we are most grateful for in life, rarely does a tangible object make it to the top of our list. Our relationships and experiences are what we treasure.

Think of the people you encounter on a daily basis. Isn't it fair to say that grateful people are contented people? They are resilient and resourceful. They find silver linings. Creativity seems to flow and they are able to see the beauty in the most ordinary of experiences. Grateful people accept their challenges and revel in the possibilities. They are people who share accolades with others, allowing the spotlight to shine on everyone. Grateful people do not let misfortune stand in the way of finding gifts buried underneath the pain. They understand that it is the small things in life that really matter. Positive energy re-gifted to the world is the outcome of a grateful heart. It appreciates all of God's creation.

Gratitude begins with knowing, loving, and feeling at peace with who you are. It is recognizing where you have come from, struggles and all, and accepting each day as it comes. So often we focus our energy on our shortcomings and mistakes that we don't appreciate our God-given gifts and strengths. Our social ranking, economic earnings, and achievements make no difference to God. He's not waiting for us to become someone before we are of value to him! God simply asks us to show up and to use our gifts towards those we encounter in our day.

Michael Josephson says, "The world has enough beautiful mountains and meadows, spectacular skies and serene lakes. It has enough lush forests, flowered fields and sandy beaches. It has plenty of stars and the promise of a new sunrise and sunset everyday. What the world needs more of [are] people to appreciate and enjoy it. The world also has its share of suffering and pain. That, too, we must appreciate with open eyes and ears and giving hearts."

Try these simple gratitude exercises:

- Write down everything you experienced in the last hour. Tune in with your senses and allow yourself to relive the hour with a deeper level of awareness. What did you do and say, what actions came to mind, how did you feel? The more conscious you are of the simple and natural gifts that surround you, the more grateful your heart becomes, and the more you feel connected to God.

- Find ways to remain mindful and to express your gratitude. Begin a gratitude list, perhaps in a journal. Start by writing five things each day for which you are grateful. Some days your gratitude may focus on very ordinary experiences like being able to drink clean water or eat a nutritious meal. Another day you may be grateful for a serendipitous experience that leaves you awestruck.

- At the top of a chalkboard or whiteboard scrawl out the words: Today I'm Grateful For: See what happens to you personally or to your family and co-workers as they are invited to add to the list. You don't have to say anything; the invitation is extended in the words.

- While we may not be able to change the world, we can help

change the space we occupy in it. Jesus said, "If I, therefore, the master and teacher, have washed your feet, you ought to wash one another's feet. I have given you a model to follow, so that as I have done for you, you should also do." (John 13:14-15) Washing the feet of others is a way to express our gratitude to God for all the gifts we have been given. Here are a few examples of how we can wash another's feet:

- Speak with kind words. Avoid words that label, demean, or show intolerance toward a group or individual. We build up God's community by not tearing people down.

- Act with a kind heart. Someone's poor disposition, bad day, or unbearable attitude is an opportunity for you to let your light shine in a dark space.

- Take time to pray for others. Rather than focusing on outcomes, pray that God's will be accepted in all circumstances.

- Be present. Listen with your heart. Allow silence to heal.

- Give joyfully of your talents, creativity, capabilities, and treasures. The simplest gifts are those we treasure most.

- Expand your capacity to love. What we offer to another in sacrifice creates a joyful heart in us. Do something everyday that demands no payment of any kind.

- Intervene when you see injustice. Speak up. Pay attention to your gut instincts and the values you learned growing up. It's easy to follow along, yet in the end, disquieting to live with an unsettled conscience.

- Touch people. We have a tradition in which we extend a sign of peace to one another at Mass. It is in the touching of flesh with flesh that we meet God in one another.

- Give alms. Serve the poorest among us. By serving those in need, we honor and thank God.

- Invite people to the table. We evangelize not by coercion but by invitation. Encourage and invite people to share in community with you. It could be a spiritual program you are attending, a meal, an evening get-together, a picnic in the park, or a drive to

the ice cream stand. Think of people who may need companion-
ship.

- Simply say, "Thank you God for making me, me. May everything I do today serve, praise, and give thanks to you."

- Ask yourself periodically throughout the day if what you are
doing is serving, praising, and honoring God. If you can answer a
resounding, "Yes!" chances are your heart is filled with gratitude.

PERSONAL REFLECTION

How have you served, praised, or thanked God today? At any point
in this day, have you been conscious of how your words or actions
have had a positive or negative affect on someone? If negative, is
there a new perspective you can take that may facilitate changes?

Write down five things for which you are grateful today. Describe briefly
why they make you feel a sense of gratitude.

If you were able to do anything to express your gratitude toward another
person or group, who would it be and what would you do? What stops you
from doing it?

What questions, thoughts, reflections arise in you at this time?

Notes and References

Introduction
Theodore James Ryken- founder of the Xaverian Brothers in Bruge, Belgium in 1839. The Brothers are dedicated to Roman Catholic education and working alongside missionary priests in Haiti, Africa, and the U.S.

Acceptance
Jean Baptiste Girard- Swiss Franciscan Educator
Sarah Ban Breathnach- author of several books including *Simple Abundance: A Daybook of Comfort and Joy* (1995)
Gerald May- authored several books including: *Addiction & Grace* (1998), *The Dark Night of the Soul* (2004) and *The Awakened Heart* (1991) that uniquely blend spirituality and psychology.

Balance
Thomas Merton- a Trappist monk who authored more than seventy books on mysticism, poetry, spirituality, and social justice. Among those books are: *The Seven Story Mountain* (1998), *The Hidden Ground of Love* (1985), and *No Man is an Island* (1983).

Empathy
Henri J.M. Nouwen- a Dutch-born Catholic priest and writer. He authored many books, including the *Inner Voice of Love* (1998). This book dealt with his personal struggle with clinical depression. Other noteworthy books include: *Out of Solitude* (2008), *The Dance of Life* (2005), *With Open Hands* (2006), and *Seeds of Hope* (1997).

Flexibility
St. Francis de Sales – a saint in the Roman Catholic Church known for his deep faith and gentle approach toward everything and everyone he encountered. Many of his writings focused on the topic of spiritual direction and spiritual formation. *Introduction to the Devout Life* (2010), first published in 1608, was unusual in its day, as it was written especially for laypeople.

Forgiveness
Reinhold Niebur – an American Theologian and charismatic speaker who is credited with writing the *Serenity Prayer*. In 1964, he was awarded the Presidential Medal of Freedom by President Lyndon Johnson.

Generosity
Ralph Waldo Emerson – an American essayist, lecturer, and poet. He led the Transcendentalist movement in the mid-nineteenth century and his many works have greatly influenced writers and poets that followed after him.

Listening
Alice Fryling – as a spiritual director, retreat leader, and author she has devoted her life to helping others know God and themselves more deeply. She is the author of several books including: *Seeking God Together* (2009) and *The Art of Spiritual Listening* (2003).

Loving
Julia Cameron – an artist, novelist, songwriter, and poet. She has written several books including: *The Artist's Way* (1992), *The Sound of Paper* (2004), *Walking In This World* (2002), *Answered Prayers* (2004) and *Blessings* (1998). Her style is down to earth and eloquent.

Mindfulness
Thich Nhat Hanh – a Vietnamese Zen Buddist Monk, teacher, author, poet and peace activist. He travels internationally giving retreats and talks. He has published several books including *The Miracle of Mindfulness* (1991).

Openness
Sue Monk Kidd – a writer, novelist and memoirist. She recounts the beginning of her spiritual search in *God's Joyful Surprise* (1988) and her transformation at mid-life in *When the Heart Waits* (1990). She has also authored several other books including: *The Secret Life of Bees* (2002) and *The Mermaid Chair* (2005).

Patience
Rainer Maria Rilke – an Austrian-born poet and novelist who traveled extensively through Europe and North Africa, eventually settling in Switzerland. His work was often described as "mystical." His poetry explores the Christian

search for God and the nature of prayer.

Prayer
Joseph F. Schmidt – a Christian Brother, lecturer and spiritual director. He has written several books on St. Therese of Lisieux including: *Everything Is Grace: The Life and Way of Therese of Lisieux and Praying with Therese of Lisieux* (2007). He also authored *Praying Our Experiences* (2008), which helps us to pray by bringing God into the ordinary experiences of our lives.

St. Ignatius of Loyola – founder of the Jesuits and a spiritual leader in the Catholic Church. He experienced a deep conversion of faith and followed the example of spiritual leaders such as Francis of Assisi. He formulated the fundamentals of the *Spiritual Exercises*, a compilation of meditations, prayers, and contemplative practices that help people deepen their relationship with God.

William Blake – an English poet, painter and printmaker. Although his work was largely unrecognized during his lifetime, he is now highly regarded for his expressiveness and creativity, and for his philosophical and mystical writings.

Responsibility
Joe Klaas – author of many books including: *The Twelve Steps to Happiness.* (1982). His books have helped people to find health, happiness and recovery from compulsive disorders and addictions.

Surrender
A.W. Tozer – an American-born Christian pastor, preacher and author. Born into poverty and self-educated, he later authored over thirty books including *The Pursuit of God* (1982) and *The Knowledge of The Holy* (1978). His preaching and writing were extensions of his deep and faithful prayer life.

John Phillip Newell – a poet, peace-advocate and minister. He is acclaimed for his work in the field of Celtic Spirituality. He travels internationally and speaks on themes related to the sacredness of the earth and oneness of the human soul. He has published several works including *Listening for the Heartbeat of God: a Celtic Spirituality* (1997), *Celtic Treasure: Daily Readings and Prayer* (2005), *Ground of All Being* (2008).

Teachability
Ronald Rolheiser – a Roman Catholic priest and member of the Missionary Oblates of Mary Immaculate. He is a writer and lecturer. He has written several books and writes a weekly column carried by newspapers worldwide. His books include *The Holy Longing* (1999), *Our One Great Act of Fidelity* (2011), and *The Incarnation: Keeping God In The Flesh* (2012).

Holman Hunt – an English painter who emphasized the natural world and spiritual devotion to truth. His paintings are vivid in color, pay attention to detail, and are deeply symbolic. Paintings include: *The Light of the World* (1854), *The Finding of the Savior in the Temple* (1860), and *The Shadow of Death* (1871).

Vulnerability
Madeleine L' Engle – An American poet, story- writer and journalist. Her book, *Bright Evening Star* (1977), is a memoir that tells the personal story of her faithful journey to know Jesus. In *And It Was Good* (1983), she shares observations about creation and the Creator. She wrote a children's prayer book entitled *Anytime Prayers* (2000).

Willingness
Meister Eckhart – a German theologian in the Dominican Order. He was a philosopher and mystic. Widely dismissed for centuries, interest in his work was revived in the early nineteenth century. Eckhart's sermons were inspiring. He encouraged his listeners to empty themselves of ego and things and place God at the center of their being.

Bibles
There were several Bibles referenced for scripture quotations. These included
The Rye Study Bible (1976),
The New American Bible (1986), and *The Life Recovery Bible* (1998).

Notes and References

There are several authors that have inspired and influenced my work over the years. I've listed a few below, along with my favorite books:

Paula D' Arcy – *Gift of the Red Bird* (1996); *Red Fire* (2003).

Melody Beattie – *Journey To The Heart* (1996); *More Language of Letting Go* (2000).

Rick Carson – *Taming Your Gremlin* (2003).

Joan Chittister – *Called To Question* (2004); *The Story of Ruth* (2000); *The Gift of Years* (2008); *40-Day Journey* (MN, 2007).

Susan Conroy – *Mother Teresa's Lessons of Love & Secrets of Sanctity* (2003).

Thomas Green – *Darkness in the Marketplace* (1981); *Weeds Among the Wheat* (1984).

Margaret Guenther – *Holy Listening: The Art of Spiritual Direction* (1992).

James Martin – *My Life with the Saints* (2006); *The Jesuit Guide to (Almost) Everything* (2010); *Between Heaven and Mirth* (2011).

Timothy Radcliffe – *What Is the Point of Being A Christian?* (2005); *Why Go To Church?* (2008).

Richard Rohr – *Breathing Underwater* (2011); *Radical Grace* (1993); *Falling Upward* (2011); *Simplicity: The Freedom of Letting Go* (1991).

Joyce Rupp – *The Cup of Life* (1997); *Out of the Ordinary* (2000); *Inviting God In* (2001); *The Cosmic Dance* (2002); *The Circle of Life* (1997); *Open Door* (2008).

Thomas Ryan – *Four Steps to Spiritual Freedom* (2003).